enough!

enough!

· · · · · · · · · · · ·

How to Liberate Yourself and Remake
the World with Just One Word

LAURIE McCAMMON, MS

Conari Press

This edition first published in 2016 by
Conari Press, an imprint of
Red Wheel/Weiser, LLC
With offices at:
65 Parker Street, Suite 7
Newburyport, MA 01950
www.redwheelweiser.com

ISBN: 978-1-57324-683-5

Library of Congress Cataloging-in-Publication Data
Names: McCammon, Laurie, author.
Title: Enough! : how to liberate yourself and remake the world with just one
  word / Laurie McCammon, MSAEd.
Description: Newburyport, MA : Conari Press, 2016. | Includes bibliographical
  references and index.
Identifiers: LCCN 2015047184 | ISBN 9781573246835 (paperback)
Subjects: LCSH: Conduct of life. | Values. | Simplicity. | Spirituality. |
  BISAC: SELF-HELP / Personal Growth / Self-Esteem. | SELF-HELP / Personal
  Growth / Happiness. | SELF-HELP / Motivational & Inspirational.
Classification: LCC BJ1589 .M3296 2016 | DDC 158.1--dc23
LC record available at http://lccn.loc.gov/2015047184

Cover design by Jim Warner
Cover photograph © image source / image source
Interior by Howie Severson
Typeset in Goudy Old Style

Printed in Canada
MAR
10 9 8 7 6 5 4 3 2 1

To all who agreed to be here at this auspicious time for the reawakening of the heart of humanity.

Contents

Introduction   xv

PART ONE
Where the Enough Message Came From   1
    Chapter 1: Together We Rise!   3
    Chapter 2: The Enough Message   13
    Chapter 3: A Brief History of Enough   37
    Chapter 4: Where Can Enough Be Found?   53

PART TWO
Using the Enough Message to Benefit
Ourselves and the World   77
    Chapter 5: I Am Enough   79
    Chapter 6: I Have Enough   127
    Chapter 7: We Are Enough   143
    Chapter 8: We Have Enough   175
    Chapter 9: Enough!   193

PART THREE
Invocation of the New Story   211
    Chapter 10: The Enough Story Has Begun   213

Invocation   223

Acknowledgments   225

Bibliography   229

e•nough

iˈnəf/

> *synonyms:*
>
> sufficient
>
> plenty
>
> a sufficient amount
>
> an adequate amount
>
> as much as necessary

The Enough Message

I am enough.
I have enough.
We are enough.
We have enough.
Enough!

Is scarcity inevitable?

Could humanity be the last to know that scarcity is a myth?

Introduction

*The only true voyage of discovery, the only fountain of Eternal Youth,
would be not to visit strange lands but to possess other eyes, to behold
the universe through the eyes of another, of a hundred others, to behold
the hundred universes that each of them beholds, that each of them is.*

—Marcel Proust

I was in my late twenties when I first heard the anecdote of the boiling frog. The story goes like this: If you boil a pot of water, then put a frog in, he will jump right out, saving himself. But if you put a frog in a pot of cool water and slowly turn up the heat, he will not sense the changes that are happening and will remain in the pot to boil to death. While actual frogs have been proven to not act in this manner (saving themselves no matter whether the heat is turned up slowly or quickly), what I've come to understand is that we, the people on Earth at this time, are the frogs in this story. The heat, in the form of economic inequity, security concerns, environmental disruption, and various other factors has been turned up slowly and steadily over decades.

I certainly could begin this book by recounting the disturbing conditions present today, but I'd like to ask your permission to skip that step, feeling we have already been traumatized enough by all the tales of suffering and destruction. The preponderance of evidence pointing to a crisis is clear, as is the growing consensus that approaching the problem from the level of symptoms, or even of behaviors, will not be nearly enough. What we are told may be enough is a transformation of consciousness, a global paradigm shift. But how can we possibly get there, and together? Are we as a humanity smart enough, creative enough, flexible enough, collaborative enough, spiritually and emotionally mature enough to make such a leap?

Yes, yes we are. It is already happening. By the time you finish this book, you too will see that it is already happening in you and all around you.

I will admit that it is an exceedingly difficult time to be alive. I don't think that the gap between what we feel is "right" inside and what is reflected in the world at large has ever been greater. But if we think about it, this points to a key opportunity. The reason for the widening gap is not just that conditions on Earth are in steady decline, but also that human consciousness has been evolving and expanding beyond where it has ever been before. What we have at present isn't an unstoppable slide into a death spiral, it is a pulling apart of two realms: the existing world, and the universe we carry inside of us as unrealized potential and unexpressed wisdom. Which will we believe in? Which will we stand up for? Which will we invest in? As long as the old world was a convincing enough story (or close enough to convincing), it had the power to command our loyalty and attention and make us doubt the inner story. As long as we trusted the outer world to have our own best interests in mind, there was no need to turn to the universe within. All of this has changed.

Certainly, many of us are too busy, tired, overwhelmed, or disempowered to pay close attention to the widening gap between the inner and outer realities, but I believe it is a shared human experience to sense a global dissonance and to register an internal discomfort about it. Feeling the dissonance can put into motion a self-preservation response that comes out sideways as anger, violence, impatience, frustration, hopelessness, fierceness, grieving, hoarding, addiction, escapism, or depression. It is easy to place the blame for these uncomfortable emotions on our individual circumstances or to see them as expressions of personal weakness or flaws. It is easy to feel we are alone in wrestling with such demons. But please don't believe it for a second. If this Enough work has taught me anything, it is that something much bigger and more universal is going on, something we are here to understand together.

I imagine that you feel an inner calling, however faint or strong, to do something about the less than ideal outer world. You sense that the story being played out by mainstream culture is not aligned with who you really are. It is damaging Earth. It is keeping people in a state of separation, lack, and fear. It is heartbreakingly unnecessary. Perhaps you are awaiting a hero or mass movement to do something about the flawed mainstream story. Perhaps you are waiting to meet more people who think like you do. Perhaps you are awaiting a sign to more deeply trust what you already know. If so, I promise you that you will find comfort and resolve within this book. The awareness growing in you is real. Partners are waiting. New leadership is emerging. Inspired practical solutions are rising to the top. You are not alone. *You are one who sees.*

"We who see" understand things that the mainstream story does not talk about. We know that we can affect reality by changing our thoughts. We realize that not only are we powerful manifestors of our reality, but that something collective is occurring in which our contributions are interconnected with others', causing a kind of acceleration and expansion. The existing worldview with all its core assumptions and rules has stretched all it can to try to contain our growing consciousness. We seem to know that, like the frogs in real life, nature has imbued us with the means to thrive amid this or any crisis. Sensing the danger is only the first step. Crisis awakens something unexpected and deeply powerful within us, a hidden and untapped potential. This is the part of the story we do not talk about in public. But it is and always has been the true "lead story." This is the Enough Story it is my purpose to tell. It isn't a new story. It is the most ancient of all stories. It is as old as the universe itself, and it keeps repeating itself again and again. Perhaps if I begin with a very old story, you will see what I mean.

As the old story goes, a Mayan shaman was the first to see Spanish boats approaching the shore and warned his people about an impending time of great change. Try as he might, he could not find anyone from his tribe who could physically see the ships. It had never happened before. There was no context for understanding such visions, no way for them to integrate the idea of "people from across the sea" into their view of how the world works. The shaman, on the other hand, had worked with visions and dreams all his life. He knew that the tribe's interpretation of the world did not capture the ultimate truth. He knew that paradigms and worldviews were temporary constructs of the mind, created to be outgrown. Consciousness, he knew, was the only truth, an ever-expanding stream that stretches from the beginning of time, revealing a more precise truth as time goes on. In touch with these intangible and subtle knowings, he was able not only to see the unexpected in plain sight, but also to instantly understand its impact on the future of his people. The arrival of the ships meant nothing less than the end of one way of life for his village and the beginning of the next.

On Earth today, there are exponentially more of us working intentionally with visions and dreams, many more of us tapped into a personal knowing that our global culture is undergoing another such rebirth, a major departure from an existing way of life. I will not call this capability spiritual or mystical, as this places it into too small a conceptual box. It is so very much more than that. In many ways, what we see gathering on the horizon is the sequel to the Mayan shaman's story. The shaman was announcing a time when a new paradigm of materiality, hierarchy, and bravado would take over the world. We are experiencing the imminent breakdown of that very paradigm now. It is a paradigm that has run its course. We have an opportunity in our present era to release that difficult chapter to the past and to embrace a better one. With advances in science, technology, and spiritual understanding, we have the opportunity to embody the path of the shaman—to see and know so much more about our human destiny and future.

In 2011, I experienced a vivid dream. In the dream, I found myself in a strange and mystical land. A regal woman stood before me wearing flowing white robes and beautiful jewelry that I could tell meant something about her position. She motioned for me to follow her and we ascended a path up a steep hill. About halfway up the hill, she gestured toward a large pool of water in the ground and asked me to bathe in it. I followed her instructions and looked up to find one of her assistants offering me new clothes. As I dressed, I noticed that the clothing and jewelry I was putting on were the very same I had earlier seen on the woman. She had disappeared from view. I realized in an instant that I had somehow *become* her. I continued up the hill, a growing sense of urgency and purpose buoying my steps.

At the top of the hill, the land was flat and arid, a profoundly peaceful, spiritual place. Perched before me was a huge round, open-sided building held up by massive stone columns, similar to a Greek temple. Nearly a hundred men and women dressed similarly to me were assembled inside, taking seats on cushions along the edge of a large, circular ledge at the center of the building.

I realized I was there to report to my colleagues about the current conditions on Earth. The room went silent as I took my turn to speak. As I did so, I felt welling up in me the unshakable conviction that comes from extensive field research. "The men and women of Earth need more information. Things are very bad right now. Please, we must give them more information." The room went abuzz as people discussed this option amongst themselves. The answer came swiftly. My request was granted. I woke up with a start, experiencing an immediate sense of relief knowing that help was on its way. But more information . . . what could that mean? What kind of information?

It had never occurred to me that I could possibly be the receiver and the conveyor of a piece of the information I had requested in the dream. I had assumed it was someone else's job, but "more information" did come through me unexpectedly just a few months later. When I figured out my assignment, I chuckled nervously, "Wow, I should be *way* more careful what I ask for!" But perhaps if I had realized ahead of time that this book would be my assignment, the perception of my own inadequacy in light of such a huge task would surely have frozen me in my tracks. I had not written a book before. I had not spoken out so publicly before. How could I be up for the task? What I do know is that we aren't being rescued and I am not being asked to serve as a rescuer. That is an outdated way of looking at our planet's predicament. What is happening is that we are being given more information to assist us in rescuing *ourselves*.

The information I received was what I call the Enough Message, and it was so surprisingly profound that I have devoted three years of my life to studying it and going through my own Enough initiations in order to embody it. What I know now is that the Enough Message is the answer to my prayer for the people of Earth. It is timely and precise, meant to guide each of us safely and triumphantly through these trying times of global breakdown-breakthrough. I think it may well give us what we need individually and collectively to leapfrog into the world we always knew was possible, the world we truly want, the world I now know we are imminently qualified to create from our current level of consciousness.

It is my assignment and responsibility to share this information with you, my sisters and brothers of Earth. It is your assignment, if you wish, to use it to liberate yourself, and by doing so, to breathe life and momentum into the emergence of a new world.

Part I

Where the Enough
Message Came From

*Could it be describing the
emerging planetary story?*

~ 1 ~
Together We Rise!

Three years ago, I received the five-sentence Enough Message. Although it stood out in certain ways, downloads like this weren't all that unusual for me. I had received messages before. I started to refer to them as "divine downloads," as they differed from my own thoughts in ways that were easily recognizable by their unique energy and their rapid, uninterrupted flow. Whatever form these encounters took—a song, a poem, a phrase, a whole story—they were always accompanied by a soft feeling I can only describe as love—expansive, benevolent, deeply connected, and nurturing. I would feel a kind of ripeness in the moment and that would be my signal to just relax and pay close inner attention. Then something would begin to flow through. I by no means feel that I am special to receive these messages. On the contrary, I think the ability to do so is much more commonplace than many of us would care to admit. These experiences defy logical scrutiny and contradict the widely accepted idea that we are alone and separate. We seem to be much more comfortable labeling them as rare and special, an aberration, something only certain people can experience. But as I will reveal in multiple ways throughout this book, these messages are anything but rare or restricted. They are an integral part of who we are, proof that we are and always have been much more than enough.

We are currently living in what I call the Never Enough Story, a cultural myth characterized by ideas of separation, unworthiness, and scarcity. It is a culture that indoctrinates each and every one of us to the idea that we are separate, on our own, and there is never enough to go around. By extrapolation, this also means *we* are not enough, and we never will be. We are taught to believe that we are flawed beings, lacking in talent, perseverance, initiative, discipline, or wisdom. We must strive to overcome our inadequacies. We must work to prove we are worthy; prove that we can compete and win. We must also exchange precious time and energy to accumulate material objects that will serve as tangible proof to the world of our worthiness.

This is the Never Enough culture creating an illusion of a less connected, less abundant, less helpful universe than I know actually exists. What I know is that we are far more precious, divine, wise, and gifted than we allow ourselves to believe. What I know is that we do not need to be manipulated, tricked, or coerced into being productive or "good." If we were completely free to choose, it would be our greatest joy and our most natural impulse to bring maximum value to the world.

Divine Inspiration: Our Hidden Source of Abundance

Why do I believe human beings are inherently good? Many famous thinkers and artists throughout history—Socrates, William Shakespeare, Johann Sebastian Bach, Thomas Jefferson, Albert Einstein, Nikola Tesla, and John Lennon, to name a few—have openly acknowledged a direct connection to divine source. Both the ancient Greeks and Romans had a word to describe the "spirit," which they believed spoke to people and brought them in-spir(it)-ation. The Greek term for this, *daemon*, has since been associated with evil, while the Roman term, *genius*, has been reduced to refer only to one's IQ. If the original translation of these terms had been preserved, we would recall that divine inspiration requires no effort and is not earned. It is freely offered to anyone who is open to receiving this connection. This important detail is central to understanding the Enough Message, because the abundance we seek can be found in subtle and deeply subjective places that the Never Enough culture would never take seriously. And yet, the survival of our species may depend on us taking these sources very seriously. We are enough to solve any practical problem before us because the fullness of who we are includes divine in-spir(it)-ation, our ability to source unanticipated grace and genius directly. It is the hidden key, our ruby slippers.

A Word with a Hidden Message

As a poignant example of how transformative, timely, and surprising the Enough Message can be, as I was writing this book, it occurred to me that it was incredibly bold to write a book about one word without investigating its etymology. As illustrated by the words *daemon* and *genius*, learning the origins of a word can reveal enlightening information that has been hidden for a very long time. I had hoped this would be the case with enough.

I couldn't have been more delighted about what I found: In the original meaning of the word *enough* was a crystal clear pronouncement of humanity's collective liberation! *Enough* has its roots in the 1300s Old English word *genog*, which is a compound of *ge-* meaning "with, together" and *–nah*, "to reach or obtain." In Hittite, the root is *–ninikzi*, which means "lifts, raises."

Together we rise!

Together with divine inspiration. Together with one another. This points to our inherent enoughness as beings who are inseparable from and essential to the whole of humanity, the whole of nature, and the whole of spirit. We belong to one another, to Earth, to the whole that can never be complete without us. We are enough because the whole to which we belong is and always has been enough. We are recovering the deep sense of belonging that has been stripped away from us by the narrow-sighted Never Enough cultural paradigm. The Enough Message is coming to the surface of our collective consciousness to assist us in understanding the scope and dynamic of humanity's planetary transition. The days of the lone wolf are over. We belong. We are enough. Together we rise!

Leaving no doubt of "Together we rise!" was the unique circumstance in which the Enough Message came into my life. I had always received divine downloads when I was alone and considered them private messages, but the Enough Message appeared while in the presence of Ann Landaas Smith, a leader in the women's circle movement. As the message came through me, it did so with a tremendous amount of energy. Ann felt it and reacted in a way that told her the Enough Message hit an important and timely chord and needed to be shared. Ann is a woman of action. She has served as a delegate to the United Nations Commission on the Status of Women for thirty years. As the former director of International Women's Programs for the Episcopal Church, she had accumulated a global, multicultural perspective about what women need and want and what it takes to empower feminine leadership. Her presence with me in that moment was no accident. I got the message. *Together we rise!*

It took me about a week to gain clarity about my role in serving the Enough Message. I would write about it. As I worked with the Enough Message, it became a compelling mystery to unfold. It had much deeper layers than its initial simplicity revealed. Those deeper layers surfaced through an organic blend of synchronicities, research, scientific data, help from others, and divine guidance. I very soon realized that volunteering for this assignment meant that I would become just as much a student of the Enough Message as an interpreter.

We Are Learning to Right Ourselves

I am happiest when I am thinking outside the box, looking for connections between science and spirituality, the head and the heart, the indigenous and the innovative. My tools are just as likely to be meditation, a walk in nature, and deep listening as research, story collection, and data analysis. I believe this is the kind of full-spectrum work that a shift of paradigms asks us to do. We look for meaning amid the chaos and breakdown. We find the steady cord of aliveness tugging at the human spirit, urging us onward and often into unexpected places of the heart, body, and mind.

What I have come to understand is that when the mainstream only consults the intellect without also consulting intuition and heart-knowing, we miss a great deal of the picture. Intuition, our innate capacity to sense solutions from a holistic, instantly knowing perspective, looks too effortless to garner the respect of the Never Enough establishment. And yet, heads without hearts are what have gotten us into messes such as climate disruption, war, poverty, and ecosystem collapse. Heads without hearts cannot perceive wholeness, and tend to assume we are not responsible to a larger, interconnected, and interdependent family of living beings. Our gridlocked political and economic systems have revealed their inability and their unwillingness to serve the well-being of the whole. When the information we use to make decisions is referenced only from the same old Never Enough mindset, we can only repeat the errors of the past rather than create the world we truly want.

Luckily, the entire world, including human consciousness, is constantly evolving. What passed our notice yesterday piques our interest and invites scrutiny today. Everywhere we see evidence of humanity breaking through the boundaries between the head and the heart. Quantum science is a leader in this understanding and has confirmed we are connected at all times with the vast intelligence of the universe. For example, we've learned that something like a "big bang" occurred not only once at the birth of the universe but also occurs at the quantum level each time nonlocal energy becomes a "solid" particle in a flash of light, underscoring that the seen and unseen are part of a larger nested process that we are only beginning to comprehend.

We are also just beginning to understand the profound intimacy we share with this larger nested system. Scientists have confirmed that the big bang process occurs in our own brains when a neuron fires. A thought arises from the nonlocal plenum and through the firing of unique patterns of neurons in the brain (big bangs) creates a new a thought form "from nothing." When we have a novel thought or insight, and then act upon it, we literally are creating form from formlessness, directly and intimately acting as co-creators of something entirely new in the universe. This is why, when asked the location of the center of the universe, a quantum physicist is likely to say, "Everywhere!"

Quantum physicists discovered another amazing fact: When they conducted the famous double-slit experiment with quantum particles, they noticed that the behavior of the particles and where they appeared were influenced by the presence of a human observer. What is known as the observer effect in quantum physics reveals that the world is not made up of autonomous particles suspended in empty space. What we had previously thought of as empty space separating observer and observed is actually teaming with consciousness, a virtual network of energy and information exchanges that connect the observer and the observed. We are far more magical and inwardly abundant than we realize, hardly the lowly, disempowered, "not enough" creatures we have been taught to believe that we are. Clearly, a deeply intimate co-creative relationship with the cosmos is baked into us as human beings, one we have yet to fully utilize.

A Heart-Led Revolution

A paradigm shift is an incredibly significant thing. By all accounts, we have not had a major paradigm shift in over five thousand years. Two hundred generations is plenty of time to develop amnesia about what came before our current paradigm. It is not surprising, then, that we would make the perceptual error of assuming that the Never Enough Story is the only story humanity has ever lived or ever could live. We owe an incredible debt to the indigenous wisdom keepers who have preserved the stories of a much older paradigm. Through their perspective as well as that of cutting-edge science, we are realizing that in terms of the 13.8-billion-year-old universe story, as well as the 4.4-million-year-old hominid story, the very new 5,000-year-old Never Enough Story represents only an infinitesimal blink in time, not the big story or the only story at all.

What story will come next? We tend to expect that something as big as a paradigm shift must involve a drawn-out and perhaps violent revolution. I don't believe this has to be the case at all. These expectations come from within a Never Enough mindset and not from the broader understanding that the Enough Message offers. The emerging paradigm is not just the next in the long string of revolutionary power shifts we have seen over the course of millennia. The Enough paradigm is a different story entirely, one that does not create change through violence, war, power, competition, tribalism, and force, but negates these less evolved tendencies through a greater awareness of love and interconnectedness. Enough is very much a quiet heart-led revolution arising from the inside out, and this is perhaps why it has taken us so long to recognize it as a revolution. Many will not see it coming and will be surprised to find out who will lead the change.

What the Enough Message has taught me is this: We are a whole which is perpetually reaching toward a more profound and loving awareness of itself, a formerly Never Enough culture waking up to its much broader, ever-present roots in Enoughness. As we welcome expanded heart awareness, the answers that come to us are increasingly holistic and collectively harmonious. They are natural and loving. They unlock our joy, creativity, and sense of belonging. We are enough to awaken to our full potential as co-creators of the better world we imagine. This is the mission of the Enough Message. It is my assignment. I hope it may, in some way that is completely unique to you, become your assignment as well.

A Message to the Reader

Throughout this book, *Enough* capitalized will represent the information contained within the Enough Message. Terms such as the Enough Story, the Enough Message, the Enough worldview, and the Enough paradigm will be used interchangeably and all mean the same thing: the New Story for humanity described by the Enough Message. I will also capitalize the terms *Never Enough* and *Not Enough* and use them to denote the old worldview, old paradigm, or Old Story that is breaking down. When *enough* appears lowercased, it indicates that it is being used simply as an adjective, as in "enough said."

I begin several chapters with a quote. If I have not attributed it to anyone, it has been excerpted from this book.

❧ 2 ❧

The Enough Message

We are not hopeless optimists but humanity's best hope.

When I received the Enough Message, it streamed in as five rapid-fire sentences:

I am enough.

I have enough.

We are enough.

We have enough.

Enough!

It *felt* profoundly right. But why? How was it different from a pleasant mantra? I could feel the skeptic in me creeping in. It appeared in the form of Stuart Smalley, the *Saturday Night Live* self-help character popularized by comedian Al Franken, saying in a folksy accent, "I'm good enough, I'm smart enough, and dog-gone it, people like me." After I stopped giggling at the image of Stewart, I could not deny that the Enough Message had been accompanied by an instant feeling of profound recognition, a kind of "home signal." But why? A timely statement from one of *Enough*'s earliest supporters, filmmaker Cheryl Gould, kept me from doubting, urging me to stay awake to the deeper knowing that this message is important and to be taken seriously: "Your work will crack the code of the sleeping consciousness." I could feel the truth of that even though I didn't have the faintest idea I—or any of us—had been asleep.

When a new idea is presented to me, I have learned to apply what Buddhists call beginner's mind, something I started to do more consciously as a result of my graduate training in transformational learning. A basic tenet of transformational learning is to open oneself to new perspectives without prejudging. After receiving sufficient experience and information through a "What if this is true?" attitude and a hands-on approach, one discerns if the new perspective is useful or not, transformative or not. More than understand the words of the Enough Message, I could *feel* them. I felt an incredibly loving and urgent nudge. When I feel something this strongly, I know to stay open to exploring it further. I remembered that the last time I felt this was from experiencing a profound spiritual download years before. In that experience, a beautiful and benevolent energy had poured into my body from the top of my head like a shower of loving light. I knew the Enough Message, which felt similar, could be trusted. In contrast, the usual usage of the word *enough* had the feeling of something harsh, unkind, dismissive, and prescribed: "You are *not* enough!" There was such a difference between these two feelings. Enough without the "not" felt so much better.

It did not escape my notice that the messages we hear so often in our society about not being enough are precisely the opposite of those laid out by the Enough Message. The old familiar messages could be characterized as this: "You are not enough, so you must try to become enough through your achievements and possessions. Other people are not your helpmates but are your competitors. Remember, it is a dog-eat-dog world out there. If you do not grab your enough, someone else will get it instead of you. You must abide by these rules of engagement even when you are exhausted and spent. You will take whatever life throws at you, and you will tolerate it because this is the way life is. Life is not fair or easy, and you get what you pay for, not what you deserve."

I noticed that the core belief underlying all of this is that there is never enough—never enough time, money, natural resources, love, luck, or what have you. We are never enough, seen more for the roles we play and the things we have than for the essence of who we are. Life is reduced to a heartless, mechanical transaction of exchanging our time and labor to obtain something we think we need. From this cultural message, there is no sense of being inherently supported or unconditionally loved. We barely know what it feels like to receive without having to first earn it in some way. And yet, when the Never Enough lens is all we've known, we accept its heartbreaking limitations as "just the way things are."

The Enough Message offers up a kinder, more loving and connected reality. We align with the bigger and deeper story of who we are: We are enough just as we are. Spurred by the Enough Message, I began to notice evidence of the non-transactional Enough Story all around us—in ancient stories told by indigenous wisdom keepers, in the story of nature, quantum science, social movements, and random acts of kindness.

Could Our Cultural Story Be Making Us Sick?

The most obvious antidote to something harmful is to apply a dose of its exact opposite. Was this what the Enough Message was trying to offer—a cure for the Never Enough paradigm? It seemed logical enough, so I received my first assignment: test the hypothesis that the Enough Story is the cure to the massive suffering of the Never Enough Story. Inherent in this hypothesis is the assumption that our cultural story has made us sick; that the Never Enough Story is to blame for violence, war, exploitation, prejudice, greed, and environmental destruction. Could a belief in scarcity or lack be so pervasive, so strong, so disturbing that it could alter human behavior from what would be considered natural or life-sustaining? Could the fear of not having enough drive us to do the otherwise unthinkable? I believed so, but to prove it I began looking for evidence amongst the 8.7 million species on Earth for any kind of pervasive pattern of Never Enough behavior inherent in nature. I did not find a single case of a species that predominantly lived by a Never Enough principle, but instead found scientific evidence debunking the commonly held assumption that humanity's behavior is a natural case of "survival of the fittest."

What became increasingly apparent through my research was that the global Enough shift is already well under way, both culturally and within the consciousness of so many, and it looks nothing like dog-eat-dog or survival of the fittest. The pockets of aliveness represented by successful social, technical, and scientific innovation have discernable values in common, sharing an underlying optimism that "there is enough." In fact, I was overwhelmed by the enormity of hidden abundance present in our world. I believe you will be, too.

What I learned is that it is the old belief in lack that directly creates hoarding, greed, and overconsumption, becoming its own self-fulfilling prophecy. When we believe in scarcity, we create scarcity. But likewise, a core belief in Enough is a self-fulfilling prophecy of sufficiency, plentitude, resilience, and fulfillment. When we believe there is enough, there is no incentive to engage in fear-based consumption. When we believe we are enough, what we consume is tied to what we actually need, and not to compensating for a perceived inner deficit that keeps demanding to be satisfied again and again. This could actually mean that much of our consumption is directly driven by Never Enough thinking, and could be eliminated without giving up anything we really need to live happy, fulfilling lives.

When we allow ourselves, perhaps for the first time, to think outside of the paradigmatic Never Enough box, we are not hopeless optimists but rather humanity's best hope. The inspiring efforts of our fellow "Enoughers" to bring about humanity's spiritual renaissance will be shared in the chapters that follow. I believe what we are seeing is not some disorganized, random process, but evidence of a unified, cosmic transformation that is restoring our natural state as Enough beings in alignment with an Enough universe.

In the next chapter, I will share how General Systems Theory confirms the presence of this meta-pattern and predicts the emerging age of Enough. My belief is that we are inseparable from this cosmic process and are constantly, ever so gently nudged by it. Gradually, signposts appear as science, as revelation, as reclaimed ancient wisdom, as a new inspiration that feels timely and precisely right. The evolution of human consciousness has always moved us toward greater expansion, greater inclusion, and an ever more mature and loving response to life. Expansion, inclusion, and maturity: these are all characteristics of an Enough culture.

What is different about our present moment in history is that our growing consciousness can no longer be contained by the five-thousand-year-old paradigm. We have grown beyond it. Tweaks and minor adjustments no longer work. An entirely new paradigm is needed. The problems that remain to be solved are huge and complex, and, as Albert Einstein stated, unsolvable from within the same thinking that created them. What did he mean by "thinking"? I believe his statement was encouraging a new, more expansive consciousness or worldview. From a new consciousness, the problems we face today, such as war and poverty, would no longer be supported, tolerated, or perpetuated.

The Old Never Enough Story

"There isn't enough" and "You aren't enough" are beliefs so ingrained in our psyche and culture that they hold sway over far-ranging aspects of life, from how we perceive our self-worth (I am not enough) to the ways in which we are taught, governed, and allocated resources (You don't have enough. You aren't worthy unless . . .). In a competitive world, we'd be hard-pressed to find an institution Never Enough does not govern, a business it does not drive, a relationship it does not complicate with ideas such as "We don't have enough tax revenue to provide health care for every senior," "We must lay people off or keep wages down to make the company more competitive," or "You don't love me enough. I am not attractive enough. I bet you are thinking of leaving me for someone better."

As we continue to wake up to what is real and what is illusion, the old Never Enough Story is struggling for survival. Since consciousness is constantly expanding, as the general population of Earth evolve, the Old Story must work even harder to make us choose fear and constriction over love and connection. This means intentionally ramping up fear, distrust, and insecurity, which is precisely what we see in the media, whose air of negativity has become so pronounced that most people today have at least a mild case of PTSD. To keep the illusion alive, we need to be convinced of an imminent threat to our well-being, otherwise our natural sensibilities would not allow us to do things like wage war overseas, subsidize predatory banks with taxpayer funds, or destroy vast tracts of pristine land in the name of short-term economic gain for just a few.

In order for these things to happen, our perception of what is good must be turned upside down. Greed must be disguised as glamour and success: a credit score (derived from how much debt we take on rather than how much we save) is perceived as a measure of our maturity; corporatocracy is disguised as positive words like "Citizen's United" and "democracy"; peace, we are told is created by buying more guns and dropping more bombs; the lowest common denominator of behavior is packaged as shock entertainment and pop culture. No wonder we are confused! What we see is no longer what we get. If we can start to notice this insidious pattern, we can see the truth that resides beneath the misleading facade. Once our awareness is able to penetrate more deeply into what is really going on, we become more resilient and are no longer fooled by the bait and switch tactics of the Never Enough establishment.

Up until now, we've had little choice but to play along with the old system because a new paradigm hasn't yet been sufficiently defined or developed. While far from ideal, the Old Story is at least a game we know how to play. But straddling two worlds comes at a price. As the decline of the Old Story progresses, it siphons even more of our time and energy, producing diminishing returns. Thus occupied, we find it more difficult to muster the strength, imagination, and enthusiasm to invest in a New Story. At some point, a leap to the New Story will be self-evident and a tipping point will occur. But when do we take the leap, after enduring more suffering and creating more serious damage to Earth, or before? I vote for before.

Is Scarcity Real?

If a belief in scarcity is the root cause of all of our problems, it would be important to investigate if scarcity is real or manmade. I wouldn't be surprised if you are thinking, "But I see evidence of scarcity everywhere. Doesn't that mean it is real?" In comparing the human story with nature's story, what we see are two very different dynamics. In nature we see sustainable ecosystems that are inherently designed to provide enough for all the species of that ecosystem, forever. These systems are in balance, with every member of the system both giving and receiving something of value that keeps the system healthy. The story of humanity is one of extreme self-interest in which the ecosystem is seen as a resource to be exploited and used up. Human beings have operated for five thousand years as disrupters of natural, self-perpetuating systems, among other things, clear-cutting what once were complex, diverse, self-sustaining ecosystems and replacing them with heavily sprayed and watered monocrop plots that deplete the soil and lead to erosion, groundwater depletion, CO_2 buildup, and eutrophication of nearby bodies of water.

If scarcity in similar degrees is not observable in undisturbed ecosystems (and it is not), what does this tell us about scarcity? Scarcity is not some undisputable reality from which we cannot escape. It is the result of *choices* made by humankind. In choosing to put our faith in practices such as clear-cutting, overfishing, monocrop farming, heavy pesticide use, mountaintop removal, use of nonrenewable, polluting fossil fuels, strip mining, fracking, and dumping waste in oceans, rivers, and streams, we have actually been *manufacturing* the conditions for scarcity, trading what was once healthy, abundant, and alive for something that has become a chemical-dependent future dead zone. These conditions of scarcity have been used to perpetuate further belief in scarcity until scarcity is all we see and expect.

With so much manufactured scarcity, we are forced to spend a great deal of time and energy just trying to survive. We cease to see or sense nature's flawless way of creating sustainable abundance for everyone, a way that is our natural way.

What we are discovering, as we confront the culture of scarcity to its source, is that the fulcrum for change is actually not outside of us at all, but within us. Paradigms are collective agreements about how to perceive the world, that's all. Human agreements are revised all the time as we learn something new. A critical number of us now recognize that something is very wrong with our current paradigm. The story we have been telling ourselves has become a dangerous one. Our hearts, which can never completely lose our connection to nature, know a better one. Equality is natural. Kindness and respect for every living being are natural. Enough for all is natural. Scarcity is not.

It's important to bear in mind that limitation is not the same as scarcity or lack. Any self-sustaining system has rules that keep the system healthy, and keeps abundance flowing among its members. When all members agree to play by the rules and only take what they need, the system is self-renewable. Everyone gets enough. There are limits to what you can take for yourself without threatening other people's enough and the long-term health of the system itself. When we exceed the limits, disregarding others who share the system with us, and leave nothing to keep feeding the system, we are creating a future state of scarcity not just for ourselves but for the entire system. This scarcity would not exist had someone not taken the system out of balance by breaking the rules.

What we see is that many of our economic systems are built in a way that have either created a state of scarcity or assumed scarcity as a foundational condition. In such systems, it is simply taken for granted that it is fine for some to have much more than they need while many don't have enough. The global fiat monetary system is a system that accumulates scarcity over time, much like using a credit card, which counts on future revenue to pay past debts. If all you can afford to pay is the minimum payment due, more debt in the form of interest keeps snowballing, making it harder to pay the principal back. The mathematical flaws of the global monetary system don't become visible until the snowball has had sufficient time to build up. We have reached the snowball and are witnessing whole countries and regions of the world teetering on economic ruin. We see it in the form of bank failures and bankrupt cities, states, and countries. We see it in the form of corporate bailouts and home foreclosures. We see it in the form of jittery or falling stock markets. All of this amounts to real suffering brought on by a system whose very rules could have predicted this very outcome, rules that said scarcity and lack are okay. Even people who play by the rules in this system are forced over time to either work harder or receive less. Pension plans dry up. The cost of living rises for everyone. Taxes increase. Austerity measures are imposed. Public roads and bridges crumble. It's not a matter of pointing fingers at people who are lazy or greedy, or who have made poor financial choices. They did not create the rules. Everyone will feel the pinch because it is built into the math of the system itself. It is hard to believe that with all the intelligent economists in the world, this mathematical inevitability was not detected a very long time ago. Perhaps it was, but no one felt brave enough to demand we scrap the old system, universally forgive the debt, and switch to a new system that does not inevitably end in suffering and ruin. Such a major correction would require a global paradigm shift in how we perceive both debt and ourselves.

Nature does not create in this way. Nature does not accumulate debts. Nature is about sustaining balance, equal exchange, sharing, participation, and co-responsibility. Nature is about the kind of trust and flexibility that funnel resources to where they are most needed in the moment. Ultimately, nature is about how to minimize suffering and maximize well-being.

Enough: A Master Key

How does Enough relate to economics? How could it possibly ease suffering? In the course of any given day, chances are you have used the word *enough* several times. You've probably used it referring to something mundane, like "Have you had enough to eat?" or "Have you studied enough for the test?" but perhaps also for something more meaningful: "Am I enough, or will he leave me for someone else?" or "When will I ever have enough money?" or in reference to something broader: "Why isn't there enough food to feed all of humanity?" If you think about it, the word *enough* holds sway over our psyches and culture in wide-reaching and profound ways. And since it does so, might it possess an ability to transform many domains of our lives all at once? Might it possibly act as a master key to *unlock the sleeping consciousness*?

We live in an age where a cultural belief in Never Enough (scarcity or lack) creates a disempowering backdrop for our lives, setting the stage for competition over cooperation, materialism over inner growth, greed over sustainability, insecurity over trust, individualism over compassion. As we are striving with singular focus to obtain more, that which is truly meaningful gets less and less of our attention. We essentially grow a blind spot for the areas of our lives that could bring us the feeling of enough we seek. We forget to examine where the belief that we aren't enough came from, and if it's actually true. We forget to reflect on our patterns and whether or not they actually ever succeeded in bringing us the feeling of Enoughness we desired.

In her book *EcoMind* Frances Moore Lappé draws attention to the cultural blind spot created by our belief about Never Enough: that most of what we perceive as scarcity may be something else entirely, hidden waste that is created by the system before a consumer interacts with the goods and services on store shelves. Because we, the average consumer, cannot see how much abundance is squandered in the process of harvesting, manufacturing, and shipping, we do not realize that something can be done to avoid it.

In a recent TEDxDirigo talk, Zoe Weil, cofounder and president of the Institute for Humane Education, led the audience through an exercise called "True Price." She asked what the true price of a T-shirt is for ourselves as consumers, for other people, for animals, and for the environment. After going through the exercise we see that the price is much higher than anyone could ever have imagined. But rather than be disheartened by this news, we can choose to be excited that we are starting to see beyond the blind spot, able to glimpse the hidden recoverable abundance built into our systems as carelessness and waste. It is not resources or human ingenuity that we are lacking. Many ideas already exist to reuse and reduce waste, to localize production, to forge new partnerships, and to redesign products and services to bring maximum benefit with the least waste. An example of this is Partners for World Health, an all-volunteer nonprofit that collects medical supplies from health care facilities that would otherwise be discarded. These supplies are then donated to local clinics and to other countries in need, reducing waste and providing support where it is critically needed. What it took for this rapidly growing nonprofit to begin was a single person, Elizabeth McLellan, RN MPH, who noticed the hidden abundance in her workplace and believed she was enough to do something with it. This kind of seeing and doing is what Enough is all about.

The Truth Is Not Vulnerable

Perhaps it is audacious to imagine changing a belief as fundamental to humanity as Never Enough. But consider the tremendous amount of ongoing expense and effort that goes into the propaganda, political lobbying, corruption, legal maneuvering, secrecy, and advertising required to keep the blind spot in place. Anything requiring this much effort and expense to maintain is already vulnerable to change. The truth is not vulnerable. It doesn't need to be placed in a pretty package to be sold. We can feel and see its rightness personally. And despite the huge investment being made in perpetuating the Never Enough Story every day, never have there been more people breaking through it with their own social organizing, lobbying, and charitable work. These people can tell you how good it feels to be working for something so inherently satisfying and beneficial to all. All it will take is a critical mass of people to see beyond the Never Enough blind spot, to examine the "true price" of what we consume and be joyfully engaged in capturing the hidden abundance built into almost all our systems.

Taking Our Cues from the Wisdom Keepers

As we gather strength and courage to demand a different future, we do not need to stand alone. Fortunately, the Never Enough paradigm is not the only paradigm in existence on Earth today. If we want a glimpse of how an Enough culture works, we need only look to the pagan and indigenous cultures that have preserved their Enough understanding of the natural world and humanity's place in it. We owe an incredible debt to the wisdom keepers of the planet. They are teaching that it is through harmony and partnership with nature that we find our greatest peace and security. It is by working consciously and respectfully with the web of life that we secure our place in the future. Nowhere is this more familiar to us than within our national parks, places where the healing, sustaining, and reinvigorating qualities of nature have been respected and preserved for all to enjoy in perpetuity. One only need imagine a world in which there were no public parks at all to understand what we give up when we choose a paradigm that exploits and destroys nature for the profit of the few. What if there were more national parks and greenbelts? What if we connected with nature more in our daily lives? Wouldn't we be happier, healthier, more peaceful and loving in all our interactions?

Time for a New Story

When a story becomes dangerous, it is time to stop telling it. The Never Enough Story is by far the most dangerous story told on Earth today. We are being nudged by our evolving consciousness to rejoin the bigger story of the cosmos, the story of the universe, the story of Earth, which is a wholesome, life-sustaining story: the story of Enough.

Why Enough Is the New Story

I know it may feel that we don't have a new story yet. If we are looking to the mainstream for evidence, we will find very little of substance. New cultural stories, like water, are drawn up into the world through the grassroots. Pointing to what she had observed cross-culturally about human culture, anthropologist Margaret Mead advised, "Never doubt that a small group of thoughtful, committed citizens can change the world. Indeed, it's the only thing that ever has." So if we want to sense the New Story that is arising, we must look to the fertile fringes, to small communities of intentional and conscious people who are inventing the new Enough culture. Some of these projects, which all have the key feature of being replicable, will be featured in chapter 7.

Another way we know a new story is rising is that we are seeing an unprecedented explosion of new language and fresh meaning entering our culture: green, wellness, eco-, sustainability, thrive, Transition Town, permaculture, the sharing economy, new economics, upcycle, organic, open source ecology, global commons, social responsibility, butterfly effect, biomimicry, seven generation sustainability, and the Great Turning. Each concept in itself represents vast bodies of human endeavor, breaking through to a different way of perceiving and being. We start to see common patterns in seemingly unrelated arisings, and we start to ask if this means something ordered and interconnected is taking place. I believe it is.

Ironically, I had the opposite challenge when I encountered the Enough Message. I didn't know its purpose, only that it felt like it was supposed to serve in some way that was beyond my own self-serving needs. My graduate professor, Dr. Will Callendar, used to occasionally issue his students a challenge to "design backwards." I realized that receiving a message before I knew its purpose was exactly what he was talking about. So I filled in the blank in his frequent saying, which came out like this: "If *Enough* is the answer, what is the question?" Before I could think about it, the question came: What is the New Story? My brain remained skeptical: "Surely, if this was the case, someone else would have come up with it by now. Surely, if you investigate, you will find that it won't fit some important criterion to qualify it for such a big role. Oh, and by the way, who do you think you are, anyway? No one will listen to *you*."

The urge to get to the bottom of the Enough mystery managed to push aside considerable doubts about my own personal worthiness to do this work. I knew that to be able to trust what my heart knew about Enough, my head would need to be satisfied first. I certainly didn't mean any disrespect to the field of infinite potentiality, the collective consciousness, the *daemon-genius* from which I believed the message came. On the contrary, if humanity were to break through to a new paradigm, I believed the impetus to do so would come from the heart field and not from the intellect. The new paradigm would be understood as a field that belonged to everyone, a field that we all nurture and tend for the benefit of the greater good. I decided *the intention to serve everyone equally* would be the first criterion. I then made a list of more criteria and considered how Enough measured up:

1. Democratic: the intention to serve everyone equally

2. Simple: needs no further explanation or translation

3. Descriptive: not so general as to tell us nothing specific about the future

4. Relatable: something everyone can relate to from direct experience

5. Fractal: applicable to any endeavor, any scale, any culture

6. Causal: points to the root cause, not symptoms

7. Coherent: tells a story that links the past, present, and future

8. Natural: in alignment with natural law (as opposed to manmade)

9. Measurable: we know when we have achieved it

10. Positive and motivating: describes a desirable future

1. Democratic: The Intention to Serve Everyone Equally

Although it is true that each person's "enough" is different, the underlying intention of Enough as a new Story is to provide enough not just for oneself, but for one's community, the world, and the planet. The human Never Enough Story has been one of extreme self-interest and competition. Not only is the belief in separation a distortion of perception (we cannot exist in a vacuum), but it also facilitates unnecessary fear, violence, cruelty, exploitation, and war. The truth of Enough is that we cannot achieve well-being for ourselves without ensuring the well-being of other people and the planet. It is not Enough if we are not considering future generations and other species. We all benefit from as well as serve the ecosystem in which we live, and by doing so in a balanced way, we ensure a sustainable and just future for all.

But we do not achieve Enough for all by legislating values or by giving everyone the exact same allotment in the name of fairness. We do so first and foremost by attuning to the genuine and unique needs of each individual, including Earth. What we each genuinely need is different, so we must be willing to share in a way that in many cases means someone else will get more of a particular resource than we do. It is understanding that we as individuals are like cells in the body; we cannot thrive until and unless the whole body thrives, and that requires other cells get what they need. The desire to serve everyone equally well comes not from a feeling of selflessness and altruism, but from an intimate identification with the larger organism that is Earth and all her inhabitants.

2. Simple: Needs No Further Explanation or Translation

Nature loves simple. When something works, nature will apply it again and again in many different settings, situations, and levels of scale. For example, a spiral works for a galaxy, a hurricane, a whirlpool, a whelk, and a pinecone. In the search for something capable of universality, it needs to be simple. Applied to human endeavor, it must be so simple that it easily translates across cultures and sectors of society. Enough is eminently simple and applicable to any setting or culture—to business, education, health, energy, relationships, spirituality, religion, and government. What could be simpler than one word? The five-sentence Enough Message is easy to remember and repeat. This should help people to share it with others.

3. Descriptive: Not So General as to Tell Us Nothing Specific About the Future

Enough precisely describes what will be created: enough for ourselves, enough for our communities, and enough for the world. When a term is too generic, such as "great, new, improved," it cannot focus collective effort. There is some confusion about what it is and what it isn't. Enough is precise. With the help of real data, we can come to group consensus about what is enough. How much food is enough to feed a family of four? What size house is enough? How many hours of work per week is enough? How many acres of rainforests must we have to sustain a healthy Earth? As we create an Enough world, we will each know precisely when we have hit the mark. In contrast, a term such as New Age leaves quite a bit to interpretation.

4. Relatable: Something Everyone Can Relate To from Direct Experience

Relatability would be important because if we do not have direct experience with something, we'd have to rely on experts to explain it to us, and this would mean giving up our power. It would also imply that we, though part of this shift, were somehow not directly responsible for it. I believe we are. What makes the Enough shift so powerful is how it is felt inside our bodies first and foremost. We know our enough when we *feel* it. You cannot create what you do not feel or understand. It is by bringing our inner knowing about Enough that we are qualified to bring about a greater understanding about the nature of the *collective* Enough Story.

5. Fractal: Applicable to Any Endeavor, Any Scale, Any Culture

Place the word enough in front of anything and it works. Enough pay for women. Enough shelter for orphans. Enough water for rural villages in Africa. Enough AIDS education. Enough protections for the environment. Enough habitat for endangered species. Enough with GMOs! Enough with predatory lending! Enough with harmful pesticides!

6. Causal: Points to the Root Cause, Not to Symptoms

The Enough Message is a rewriting of our inner orientation, flipping it from Never Enough to Enough. This is change that takes place at the core level of our being, the causal level (beliefs cause behaviors). Interestingly, Enough also speaks to symptoms, which could be useful as measures of progress, but only as long as we recognize that it is the inner shift from Never Enough to Enough that is the actual fulcrum for change on every front.

7. Coherent: Tells a Story That Links the Past, Present, and Future

What I discovered about this criterion for coherency was so exciting I devoted a whole chapter to it. Chapter 3 tells two coherent stories about the history of humanity: the General Systems Theory story and the archetypal psychology story. Both of these make sense of the when and the why of the emergence of Enough in our world.

8. Natural: In Alignment with Natural Law (as Opposed to Manmade)

Evolutionary biology, ecology, and quantum science all confirm that the Enough dynamic is the core dynamic of the natural universe. Enough is a story of mutual aid, interconnectedness, and expansion. As mentioned earlier, the Never Enough Story has been ignoring abundant enoughness all over the place. Enough is a direct return to the fundamentals of natural order.

9. Measurable: We Know When We Have Achieved It

As discussed above, Enough is personally measurable. But when we work as groups, the basis for creating trust is that we can measure and negotiate its effects collectively. If it can be quantified, we will know when we have achieved it. This becomes the means for group solidarity, trust, understanding, collaboration, achievement, and, of course, celebration.

10. Positive and Motivating: Describes a Desirable Future

Enough describes a future that is secure, in which everyone's needs are met—not just the needs of "the fittest" or most powerful. It describes a shift to living by a kinder set of rules (sharing and connection). We also can envision working together to restore Earth's ability to provide enough clean air, clean water, food, and shelter for all species to enjoy. A clear and desirable vision acts as a magnet, attracting passionate action. Creating a beautiful future is inherently satisfying and motivating. Sustainability has been considered a contender to name the New Story. But if the notion is that sustainability is a moral imperative, how do you sell it to the public in a way that does not spark avoidance, shame, and fear?

I believe that any message that incites fear, even if it is backed up by scientific evidence, lacks "the right stuff" to motivate sufficient numbers of people to invest in it. Enough does not buy into the story that the future is bleak, that humanity is bad, or that we have limited time and resources to make right what is wrong. I experience Enough as a vision of abundance that includes more than what can be seen with the eye, more than we have imagined, more than we have thought ourselves capable of before. Many of the calculations we make about "running out of time" do not account for unforeseen synchronicities, sudden awakenings, and breakthrough technologies that are part of our "we are enough" natures. More importantly, change made out of shame, guilt, or fear is very different than what is possible when we are guided by vision, love, optimism, and community.

Enough is free of the heavier, darker overtones of austerity and shame. Enough inspires a sense of worthiness, self-love, and empowerment. It acknowledges a deeper wellspring of genius, compassion, and caring: "You are enough. You have enough to make a difference." Enough recognizes that if we do not feel enough inside, we will try to find our enough in all the wrong places outside. This manifests as careless waste and overconsumption. Enough does not deny that these outer actions can be destructive, but it acknowledges that their ultimate cause is an inner orientation toward Never Enough that can be shifted. When we directly address this feeling of not being enough, we no longer feel compelled to subsidize ourselves by overconsuming. I do believe this is what sustainability truly is, but unfortunately this is not how it has been presented.

What Creates Happiness

In our current Never Enough society, there is a pervasive belief that money equates to happiness. However, there is significant evidence that this is not actually the truth. Of course, those in a position to benefit from the Never Enough Story are anxious to tout many studies that have been designed to convince you that it is true. For example, the financial magazine *Forbes* presented the findings of the Legatum Prosperity Index under the heading "The World's Happiest (and Saddest) Countries." This is a study about financial prosperity, not at all a study about happiness, though the headline would cause you to automatically make that leap in perception.

The Happy Planet Index, sponsored by the New Economics Foundation, sought to get to the heart of what generates happiness and well-being. The study was designed to determine how much well-being a country receives from the amount of resources it uses, factoring in the price of consumption to today's generation and future generations as a component that affects happiness. Interestingly, the HPI found that the majority of happy countries are located in less prosperous Latin America, none of which were top scoring in the Legatum study. In the Happy Planet Index, the United States ranked a paltry 105 out of 151 countries!

Perhaps the most in-depth happiness study ever undertaken was the seventy-five-year Harvard Grant Study that followed the lives of people from childhood to old age to determine the source of well-being. George Vaillant, the Harvard psychiatrist who directed the study from 1972 to 2004, stated that the study found that acquiring more money and power doesn't correlate to greater happiness, while love and relationship do. He characterized maturity as the result of the journey from narcissism to connection. Life's inevitable challenges, when they motivate us to cultivate more connection, he said, can actually make us happier. Remembering the original meaning of enough, "Together we rise!" might Enough in all its dimensions be a far more accurate measure of happiness than money?

What this highlights is what those doing it already know: New paradigm work is deeply meaningful and satisfying. It is overwhelmingly motivated by love and vision, and not by fear or shame. Doing Enough work adds to the happiness quotient. Creating community is what happens in the process of solving problems together in more conscious and connected ways. We enrich our well-being as we enrich the lives of our neighbors. We heal ourselves as we work to heal the planet. When we help others to have their enough, the chance of feeling our own enoughness is enhanced.

❦ 3 ❦

A Brief History of Enough

A shift in the ages is a delicate and challenging time for everyone. Do we align with what we are familiar with, warts and all, or do we align with the possibility of a golden age that resonates with our aspirations but which does not yet seem real or even *possible*? In this chapter, we will share two of the most compelling pieces of evidence that the Enough age is here now as a "scheduled wakeup call," part of a much larger evolutionary process guiding our species. But to properly take in this much bigger story, we must venture outside of our regular perceptual box. General Systems Theory and archetypal psychology help us to gain a very useful bird's-eye view to better sense the metapatterns that guide our lives and our world.

How the Never Enough Story Began

Prior to five thousand years ago, the hunter-gatherer populations depended more directly on Earth. We were in essence childlike innocents, guided by the rhythms and patterns of nature. This was the time of foragers, an era when people had to work only three hours to gather a week's supply of food (in contrast to two to three days for farmers). As the practice of tending plants became more widespread, a radical new idea entered human consciousness: through agriculture, we could control the food supply and take more responsibility for ourselves. To this new culture, it didn't seem "enough" to rely on nature to provide for our needs. We were driven to improve upon nature, and went about it by destroying what was there and replacing it with farms tended by men. As we learned we could create more this way, the paradigm of Never Enough took hold. The benefits were more food than one could eat, and the ability to stay put in one place rather than migrating with the seasons. The downside was that more human labor and toil were required to duplicate what nature had previously provided with little or no human intervention. It also meant that the idea of ownership was introduced, and along with that a sense of entitlement and the need for social strata, security, and laws to bring a sense of order to a system that had many inequities built into it. Success meant a burgeoning population, and this required constant building and expansion that translated into further encroachment on the land.

You would think that agriculture would mean food was plentiful for all. Instead, author and environmentalist Toby Hemenway states that the data shows that agricultural practices actually increased bouts of famine. Evolutionary biologist and futurist Elisabet Sahtouris refers to humans as the "desert-making species" because single-crop farms destroy the land's natural ability to sustain and renew itself. The result eventually is a desert where there once was fertile land.

Discrediting Nature to Justify the Never Enough Story

The Never Enough paradigm would not have been successful in taking root had humanity been able to hold fast to its original sense of the sacredness and interconnectedness of all life. Imagine the intimacy humanity once shared with Mother Earth, how heartening it must have felt to be provided for. It was a time before separation, very similar to being a suckling baby. Humanity's trust in Mother Nature and the Enough she provided had to be called into question, and our fear and desire for separation awakened.

Earth-based religions were systematically eradicated by their more "modern" warring counterparts and their myths rewritten into warrior god and perpetrator-hero-victim stories. The mother and the divine feminine, who had been central characters in the pre-agrarian story, took on subservient or even sinister roles. Fear and shame replaced unconditional love and self-trust, making the people malleable, and the patriarchy inserted itself as a wedge between man and nature, man and divinity itself. It would have been too distasteful to exploit natural resources and one another had we kept in touch with the sacredness of nature and our innate intimacy with it. If we had retained our original sense of nature as our first and common mother, we could never slice her up, use her up, and enslave her as our property.

When the responsibility for telling the creation story was later passed from religion to science, science created a story that nature operates primarily from a predator vs. prey, "survival of the fittest" (Never Enough) ethic. This idea started to take root during the Industrial Revolution, the height of the mechanistic worldview. Survival of the fittest was used by social Darwinists to lure young men away from farms and into factories. Prior to the existence of OSHA, labor unions, and decent labor law, work in factories was so torturous and dangerous that something significant had to act as a lure. The age of materialism, competition, and greed came into fashion. Unfortunately, survival of the fittest has become ingrained in the modern culture as a social norm, something we believe we cannot overcome because surely it is in our nature to compete, even to the point of being violent.

What we find when we dig deeper is that Charles Darwin himself did not believe survival of the fittest was the primary operating system of nature or of mankind. Darwin studied how species behave when under a particular short-term circumstance, a state he called "imminent threat." He never meant his theory to be generalized to "everywhere, all the time." So what we see is the culture fabricating imminent threat as an ever-present pressure in order to keep the illusion of survival of the fittest afloat. But why? Because competition sells goods and keeps workers dedicated to their jobs. Competition and the promise of delayed reward keep us playing by the rules, even when the rules go against our innermost sensibilities. The majority of commercials and news stories project a belief that we are under imminent threat all the time, whether by the economic system, our advancing age, terrorism, disease, job insecurity, the fury of nature, our inability to attract a mate, and so on. It is only by evoking imminent threat that we can be coerced out of our natural state, which is to offer mutual aid.

We need only look as far as our own biology to see that imminent threat is not natural. Our bodies weren't built to endure prolonged periods of heightened alert. To operate in fight-or-flight mode almost all of the time is totally unprecedented amongst the species on Earth and is extremely dangerous to our bodies. As Darwin specifically pointed out, this state is reserved for small bursts when quick action is required to ensure survival.

This manufactured state of prolonged and exaggerated threat is dangerous not only to our bodies but also our psychology. The number of people taking antidepressants has soared over 400 percent in the last two decades. In the United States, 43 percent of adults take mood-altering medications daily and 42 percent of young adults regularly use recreational drugs. In 2011, mood-altering drugs accounted for $13.5 billion in sales, second only to heart drugs in total sales. Of course, it could be argued that much of the need for heart drugs is directly caused by imposed stress inherent in our "threat-alert" culture as well.

It may be highly detrimental to the human body and psyche to believe it is under threat most of the time, but it is highly useful to those in a position to exploit, sell to, and control the masses. It causes us to act in ways our bodies know are uncomfortable, to buy certain products, to give away our power, to become workaholics, to engage in escapism, and to erode our health.

An interesting and hopeful antidote to the survival of the fittest story is that Darwin's theory of natural selection has since been revised by the scientific community and is now widely referred to as the survival of the "fit *enough*."

A Story with a Happy Ending

Regardless of the tactics that wrestled the natural state of Enough away from humanity, a larger pattern can be glimpsed, one that is both reassuring and non-condemning of anyone who was complicit in shutting down Enough in the first place.

The journey from Enough to Never Enough and back again is humanity's coming-of-age story. This may suggest that there has been great value in passing through the Never Enough phase of our spiritual development. Experiencing a Never Enough culture has seeded a desire to experience its opposite, an Enough culture. Experiencing survival of the fittest has seeded a desire to experience its opposite, mutual aid.

Change is inevitable, written into the design of the psychological, biological, and archetypal stories of humanity. What are those stories, and where will they lead us?

General Periodicity

August "Gus" Jaccaci, a charismatic teacher, personal friend, and author of *CEO: Chief Evolutionary Officer* and three other books, introduced me to his life's work, *General Periodicity*, back in the 1990s. His unified theory is that everything in nature, including humanity, follows a predictable four-stage growth pattern, and that these four stages can be applied to any endeavor or scale to help explain *as well as predict* what is actually going on. Gus has worked with Margaret Mead, Buckminster Fuller, and Barbara Marx Hubbard, as well as many gifted scientists, change agents, and engineers interested in coalescing a unified theory of everything.

The concept of General Periodicity builds on Dr. George Land's 1973 work, *Grow or Die*, which outlined a three-stage growth pattern present in all nature. Gus felt a subtle but extremely important fourth step was missing, and if made explicit in the model, would benefit our understanding of how nature actually creates. I agree. To this day, I find General Periodicity one of the most useful ways of looking at the world. I have yet to find a situation to which it does not apply.

The four stages are named for the primary activity that takes place in each stage, though it is important to note that each stage is also nested, or contains some aspect of all four stages. The stages are: Gather (G) Repeat (R) Share (S) Transform (T).

Gather: This stage refers to the dynamic of something new coalescing. It can be a gathering of ideas, resources, and raw materials into a new entity, either natural or manmade.

Repeat: This stage refers to replicating or repeating the newness that was gathered in the Gather stage of growth. The focus here is on making many distinct copies of essentially the same thing or honing and strengthening something through repetition.

Share: While Repeat focuses on individuation, Share focuses on building community and interconnection. Throughout the stage of Repeat, customization and specialization naturally occur. Share is the process of embracing these differences as a larger new whole. Something new and greater is created when a system is able to draw upon more options. In Share, diversity becomes a strength. More complexity, resilience, and sophistication are possible.

Transform: After the sharing stage informs the growth process, something entirely new is learned and integrated into the system. A transformative and often unexpected potential is unleashed, a deeper awareness, a novel capability. Transform signals maturity of this particular growth pattern, clearing the way for a whole new stage in the growth process.

It is fascinating how Gus used his GRST model to map two archetypal human stories side by side—the story of human epochs (Agrarian Age, Industrial Age, Information Age, Aquarian Age) and the story of the human life span (infancy, childhood, adolescence, adulthood).

GATHER	REPEAT	SHARE	TRANSFORM
Infancy	Childhood	Adolescence	Adulthood
Agrarian Age	Industrial Age	Informational Age	Aquarian Age

© August T. Jaccaci

The really fascinating insight comes when we see in this map that humanity's current culture is expressing the adolescent phase of our species' overall story. The evidence is everywhere. Our youth-obsessed culture is not yet fully grounded and matured. We look to possessions, status markers, outward appearance, peers, accomplishments, and titles for a sense of identity and security. We are drawn to fads and cliques, the need to be popular, and are swayed by bullies and fast talkers alike. We can be self-absorbed and narcissistic, and lacking in empathy. We are subject to mood swings and are vulnerable to depression and a feeling of acute isolation. Like a teen, the modern culture is at the height of physicality and bravado and taking risks without fully considering consequences or wider, longer impacts. The modern culture is impatient and impulsive in the rush to differentiate and express. The culture tends to overestimate humanity's competence and underestimate the true complexity, vast intelligence, and underlying interrelatedness of Mother Earth.

You can find evidence of any number of these adolescent traits throughout our culture, particularly on television and in the Never Enough messages rampant in advertising. This is not to say all people in our culture are aligned with the adolescent phase of development. There is always a range or bell curve represented. Forward movement through the four stages over time is inherent in the model, which means we each are moving through GRST, just at different individual paces. It also means that some have arrived at the adult phase of consciousness already. We know that the teens who move through adolescence with the greatest ease are those who find direction from within through a passion, cause, or talent. So, too, in our adolescent society, those who attain a certain inner Enoughness become somewhat insulated from the roller coaster ride of the current epoch's adolescent volatility, freeing them to enjoy a more peaceful, happy, fulfilling existence.

On the General Periodicity map, right now the global culture is poised toward the end of the adolescent or Share phase, facing an imminent leap to Transform. This is incredibly significant because the phase shift between Share and Transform is the most challenging yet most exciting of the four-part cycle. Here is why. Gather, Repeat, and Share are sequential phases of the same process. For example, in the human life cycle, Gather–Infancy, Repeat–Youth, Share–Adolescence are all part of the process called childhood. In the gap between Share and Transform, we are asked to make a major shift of focus. In this example, Transform asks us to leave childhood behind and be an adult for the first time. At the Transform–Adulthood stage, physical development has been completed, leaving more room to focus on social, moral, and spiritual considerations. This fact portends a possible global shift away from materiality and greed.

Having experienced a separation from our initial grounding in nature in the Agrarian Age, we have sought to take nature's place as the masters of the material world. As we moved through the Repeat phase, we entered the mechanistic and scientific ages in which replication of material objects became our focus. As we entered the Share phase, the sharing of information through electronic means has become the focus, but lagging behind still are the social rules established in the Repeat phase, the primacy of individualism and competition. As we complete Share as a global society in the coming decades, we are moving toward grasping the truth that competition makes no sense. We are interconnected and interdependent. Couple this with a shift away from materialism and toward moral and spiritual development, and the world could look quite different soon.

The Enough Story Accomplishes Wholeness

What is the force that draws us forward through the four stages of growth? I believe it is a desire to experience and integrate a conscious awareness of wholeness. One GRST cycle represents the journey we take in order to grasp the whole of a particular endeavor, life cycle, or spiritual lesson. So we tend to have to experience various polarities of the same thing in that cycle. In the experience of individuation and separation is the seed of desire for its opposite, connection and unity. In the experience of materialism is the seed of desire for its opposite, the nonmaterial, or spiritual. In the experience of the Information Age is the seed of desire for deeper meaning and heart-significance. Thus we are always drawn forward, seeking the achievement of wholeness through an experience of each polarity in turn. This would explain the imbalanced nature of each age, and in particular of our current age, where individualism, materialism, information, and the masculine reign supreme while spirituality, meaning, unity, and the feminine have had to take a backseat. This would explain why the exact opposite of the current Never Enough paradigm (which is Enough) is required to reach wholeness and to complete the grand Enough/Never Enough cycle of experience.

The Transform stage of the Enough/Never Enough grand cycle means taking responsibility for ourselves and our planet in a more mature, holistic way. As our adolescent bravado fades, we grow into compassion, are able to be patient and take on the long view, build loving and empathetic relationships, understand and predict the consequences of our choices, and ready ourselves as beacons and role models of wisdom, responsibility, and stability. Why is this so exciting? What we are welcoming when we shift to an Enough worldview is humanity's long-awaited adulthood!

Archetypes and Myths

Joseph Campbell and Carl Jung made popular the investigation of myth and archetypes as ways to understand the world and humanity's place in it. The thinking is, if we uncover our core myths and archetypes, then we will have a better idea of who we are and why we are here.

The Return of the Prodigal Son

Many of the myths that resonate universally within the human psyche are a retelling of this one archetypal story: In order to appreciate our mother (in this case Mother Nature and our own internal "mother natures"), we had to leave home for a time to make our own way in the world without her. We wanted to become autonomous, to be ruled not by the emotions and intuitions of our hearts that connect us to nature and each other, but by our own independent will, intellect, and drive. But our longing for home is in the end undeniable, an itch we cannot scratch, a calling we cannot deny because it is always deep within us. We would wear ourselves out trying to find "out there" what is hidden "in here." In the end, we learn that we cannot truly find our destiny until we accept our own mother-natures as an integral and valuable part of who we are. We find our destiny the moment we turn toward home, toward our natural mother-guided roots. We are saved the moment we see, really see, for the first time through the grace of Mother Nature's unconditionally loving eyes, what we once took for granted: *that we are and have always been enough.*

This archetypal story of the prodigal son was told in the Bible, though not surprisingly, the mother was replaced in the story by a father. In the story of King Arthur and the Knights of the Round Table, the life of the knight, Percival echoes this same archetypal story line. In his youth, Percival left his grieving, widowed mother without saying goodbye, lured by the adventure of joining a brotherhood of knights, only to be obsessed later in life with retrieving the Holy Grail, something many consider a spiritual symbol for the divine feminine or mother's womb. We, like our global culture, have turned our backs on the feminine and the sacred but will seek—and find—both again.

Enough Reveals the Natural Flow

The shift to Enough is not wishful thinking and dreaming. It is the most pragmatic worldview we could possibly adopt because it is synchronized with the larger evolutionary flow of the cosmos. From the perspective of nature as one interconnected living system, Enough is the path of least resistance, the path of most flow/abundance that connects everything in harmony. It is the path of "do no harm." It is the way of grace and ease, the natural reward for providing the maximum benefit to the system that sustains us.

The old Never Enough Story, with its blindness to the universal principle of reciprocity, has reached the limits of sustainability all over the place, rapidly sowing the seeds of its own demise. In order to hide how senseless Never Enough is, those who are most heavily invested in it must turn up the dial on fear, insecurity, and paranoia in an effort to retain our attention and compliance. What they are not counting on is the enduring quality of the Enough principle, and how we each carry it inside of us as our deepest knowing, our home frequency. They are not counting on the powerful rising voice of feminine spirituality and indigenous wisdom and how together with cutting-edge science and technology we are validating and embracing intuition, receptivity, cooperation, contemplation, and natural law as the surest, most steady and satisfying way forward.

Only nature is sustainable, so ultimately the only human story that is sustainable is one that is informed by and aligned with nature. If we destroy the planet, we destroy ourselves. Earth will heal and go on. It is an Enough system. But if we insist on living a Never Enough story, we may not. It is time to confront the reckless bravado that has caused one single species in 3.7 million species to presume mastery over such an intricately balanced and complicated natural system as Earth. It is amazing given our repeated history of oil spills, soil contamination, species extinction, global warming, and nuclear fallout that companies continue to bolt confidently ahead with dangerous technologies, giving little consideration as to how to deal with long-term risks and toxic waste products that can last for over a hundred generations. So which story is *really* the more practical and realistic, the Never Enough Story or the Enough Story? Which story do you want to live in?

Humanity's Fall (Away) from Grace

Our perilous journey through Never Enough has not been wasted if we emerge now as wiser, more conscious participants in our own and our planet's evolution. We can love our journey for where it has brought us to today, leaving behind humanity's collective "dark night of the soul" to come face-to-face with our true collective potential. The Holy Grail that awaits can only be recovered by consciously seeking it. When humanity first appeared on this Earth, we were given grace from nature; then we lost it as we chose to become ever more separate from Mother Nature. This time we get to consciously choose and embody grace. Duality ceases to be the main story when we move into grace. The wants of the ego-mind cease to be the main story when we embrace that we are grace. Grace transcends duality not by denying it exists, but by using what we've learned from duality to break through to something more loving, connected, compassionate, and whole—humanity's Transform. Grace invites peace and wholeness between inner and outer, individual and collective, masculine and feminine, right brain and left brain, head and heart. Grace is a state of equanimity. This is the feeling of harmony we long for and carry in our cellular memory as a felt sense of "home." We can try and feel this equanimity here, now.

❧ 4 ❧

Where Can Enough Be Found?

The universe is made of stories,
not of atoms.
—Muriel Rukeyser

General Periodicity, mythology, and archetypal psychology all clearly point to an Enough future. But where can we expect this abundance to be found? Don't we live on a planet of diminishing resources that is burdened by overpopulation?

The Never Enough worldview is synonymous with a materialistic worldview. The assumption is that if we cannot see something, it is not there. The assumption is if we see something that looks like scarcity, it is evidence that scarcity is real and we must accept it as just the way things are and will be. The Never Enough mindset has a huge blind spot to the nonmaterial and the subtle. It sees each of us as separate and alone, not in partnership with a loving universe. It does not acknowledge the potential contained within the spiritual, the synergistic, or the vibrational. It cannot predict breakthrough technologies or new revelations of the human heart. It cannot account for the generativity of spontaneous inspiration and collective synergy. A vast amount of abundance is available to us that simply cannot be accessed from the old Never Enough worldview, an abundance beautifully evoked by the twentieth-century English poet Laurence Binyon when he said "we too should make ourselves empty, that the great soul of the universe may fill us with its breath." How do we open to the "great soul of the universe"? How do we take a deeper breath that connects us to the *all*?

I have found that Enough streams in from four primary sources:

1. You + the natural = how to live sustainably forever

2. You + the subtle = how to utilize information and energy from the quantum field

3. You + the interrelational = how to access the power and synergy of the "we" in order to mobilize global change

4. You + the vibrational = how to directly access benevolent genius and inspiration

Let's take these one by one to explore the evidence for each of these frontiers of Enough abundance.

You + the Natural

General Systems Theory is a way of looking at the world that focuses on interrelationships and interdependence within organizations, whether those organizations are physical or social. For example, a General Systems view of the human body would absolutely consider as relevant that there are ten times more bacteria within the human body than human cells. What is the relationship between human cells and the community of bacteria who together comprise the ecosystem that is our bodies? Likewise, a General Systems view would focus on the interrelationships between the community of humans and other beings within the living system that is Earth. We clearly could not exist without the air, food, and water the rest of the ecosystem of Earth provides. Humanity as part of the ecosystem of the solar system could not exist without the warmth of the sun. Humanity as part of the ecosystem of the cosmos could not exist without the raw materials contained in stardust billions of years old of which our bodies are made. We clearly, then, are part of multiple systems that extend all the way up to everything that exists. We are what Hungarian-British author and journalist Arthur Koestler referred to as "holons," something that is simultaneously a whole and a part.

As holons, it would be unwise and incomplete to act as if we could possibly exist in isolation from the systems in which we are embedded. Yet, isn't this exactly the worldview that the Never Enough Story has perpetuated? The Never Enough Story has kept us so focused on the here and now, on our own species, and on getting enough for ourselves in this present era that it has blocked us from being able to perceive the real consequences of our choices for the systems that make our lives possible. It is suicidal and therefore psychopathic to perceive our ecosystem as a commodity to be used up. But so, too, the Never Enough Story ignores the vast stores of intelligent design that are contained within the ecosystem that could teach us how to be healthy and prosperous forever. Emerging fields of inquiry such as biomimicry and General Periodicity decode nature's genius and apply it to human endeavors. They bring us back in harmony with the whole systems story of which we are a part. Contained in nature is everything we need to be able to perceive—and therefore preserve—what actually sustains life, including our own.

Pay It Forward and Give Back

We know all too well the negative environmental impact when our perception is collapsed by the Never Enough Story. But can we avoid disastrous outcomes by opening ourselves to the Enough solutions hidden in the natural world? If we did so, would we choose different behaviors? The principle of Enough means that when we are a member of a system, we can also see that we are responsible for both paying it forward to future members of that system *and* giving back to feed and renew the system itself. Therefore, the healthy response is to look upon the collective future, whether it is future generations of our own or other species or the overall state of the planet, and ask, "What do you need of me?" In contrast to the immature "me first" orientation evoked by the Never Enough Story, the Enough Story evokes a mature and connected response to life.

It is important to note that from an Enough point of view, the impetus to engage in service to Earth's ecosystem does not come from a self-sacrificing or dutiful place. Unselfish acts like martyrdom carry a presupposition of separation, one in which we deny our own needs for the sake of something or someone else, often to our own perceived detriment. What is so much richer about participating in healing the world from an Enough mindset is that we realize there actually is no separation between us and who or what we serve. The world's well-being is our well-being. We identify ourselves more and more *as* the larger system rather than as individuals with competing interests. When we heal ourselves, we are healing the world. When we heal the world, we are healing ourselves. All action to heal counts, no matter what the focus of our efforts may be. This means that meditating on a mountain may be just as valuable to healing the world as volunteering to construct a solar array to support a village in Africa. It all counts because it is all part of one emerging puzzle.

In an Enough world, there is no longer a need to hold ourselves outside of our own care, and therefore whatever activism or work we do "out there" not only can but *must* be in coherence with our inner sense of wellness and joy. Doing good in an Enough paradigm leads to freeing ourselves from cycles of karma, shame, and codependent behaviors. Doing good, when freed from these emotional entrapments, feels good. When we fall in love with ourselves as part of the unfolding miracle of the cosmos, our service to Earth comes from a natural, loving impulse to preserve precious life, including our own. It comes from the inherent knowing within that there is no long-term abundance or sustainability for ourselves or anyone else without paying it forward *and* giving back.

You + the Subtle

In a stunning demonstration of synchronicity, a friend emailed me a link to a video about the hidden abundance in the space between particles (the Zero Point Field) on the very same day I was rereading my old dog-eared copy of Lynne McTaggart's book *The Field*. McTaggart's work as an author has been to gather empirical evidence from quantum science that is useful to the average person. In light of my Enough work, one piece of information really stood out this time: What we think of as empty space or a void between material objects isn't empty at all. It is teeming with energy. The amount of energy is far beyond what we might ever imagine, 10^{40} times more than that contained in solid matter! Since it is difficult to wrap our minds around such a huge number, physicist Richard Feynman offered a description: the energy contained in just one cubic meter of space is enough to boil all the oceans of the world. Talk about hidden enoughness!

Since first reading McTaggart's book many years ago, I had become interested in Nikola Tesla, inventor, futurist, and contributor to the modern alternating current (AC) electricity supply system, and his quest to give humanity free, unlimited energy in the early 1900s. He was certain unlimited energy was available in the space between particles. The challenge was how to access this energy and convert it into a form that would be useful for human consumption. He died before giving the gift of free energy to the world, but not without contributing key technologies that harness the energy in the Zero Point Field, such as the radio and the remote control.

Although quantum physics started to overtake Newtonian physics as the predominant scientific viewpoint beginning in 1900, it is astounding that 115 years later this worldview has not yet modernized our antiquated Newtonian cultural and social belief systems. We are still largely acting as if matter is solid and that if we cannot see or touch something it does not exist. We move in the world as if the space between us and any other solid object is devoid of life and energy. We relate to ourselves as solid and separate beings, ignoring the 99.999 percent of open space contained within our very own bodies. While we remain largely ignorant of the spiritual and social implications of such facts, we've become utterly dependent on technologies that operate in the Zero Point Field, such as wireless devices, cell phones, microwave ovens, satellites, X-rays, and MRI scanners.

But if scientists and tech gurus have chosen to primarily play in the Zero Point Field, it is only a matter of time before humanity's collective consciousness will also orient toward the 99.999

percent of reality that is contained there. This has far-ranging implications for everything from environmental protection and economics to peace building. If we aren't actually separate, how do we justify harming others or denying them their enough? If we aren't actually separate, how can we allow the use of dangerous technologies such as nuclear energy or pesticides that threaten the chain of life? But what it also portends is unleashing something like 10^{40} or 99.999 percent more genius and spiritual maturity for finding solutions to every issue we face on Earth!

You + the Interrelational

After receiving the Enough Message, I came across a viral video that deeply moved me, though I didn't understand fully why at the time. It carried a similar energy to the Enough Message, so I knew to pay very close attention. It was a beautiful video of starlings flying in an autumn sky. The video showed a phenomenon called murmuration. In murmuration, thousands of birds fly millimeters away in a complex synchronized ballet, and the effect is to cause an inner shift in perception which makes us think of these thousands of birds as one huge organism that dips, twists, and dances across the sky. Why does this shift of perception move us so? What deeper truth does murmuration communicate to us without words?

We have been fascinated by geese for quite a while, understanding their V formation as a lesson in how to share leadership and how sharing the workload allows us to accomplish much more than when we work alone. Since, according to General Periodicity, we are deep into the Share phase of our human story, our attraction to the lesson of the geese makes perfect sense. Could it be that the starlings are pointing toward the imminent Transform phase, an even higher order of self-organization, one that blurs the lines between individual and group, matter and space? I believe the leap in understanding that the starlings are nudging us to see is analogous to the difference between a Newtonian and a quantum perspective.

When we try to make sense of how so many individual birds carry out such a perfectly synchronized phenomenon, murmuration looks a lot like Einstein's description of quantum entanglement: "spooky action at a distance."

It seems starlings are offering humanity a timely trigger to invite a conscious re-membering of where we are headed as human beings, a clue for how we will get there, something I call the Murmuration Code. What is the Murmuration Code? Our consciousness is expanded whenever we engage in a state of delighted wonderment. Our hearts are instantly lifted as we witness the miracle of the bird ballet, and our minds seek to understand something that defies our Newtonian models of how the world works. Our curiosity becomes a teachable moment. What are we not seeing about how the world *really* works? What are we not seeing about what is *really* possible?

At the root of any capability is a belief it is possible. So it is understandable that when mainstream biologists, embedded in the Never Enough mindset, tried to explain murmuration, they did so from a lens of seeing only the .001 percent that comprises matter and traditional biology. They concluded that murmuration must be an act of self-preservation, each bird motivated to be in the center of the pack to avoid predators. If this were an accurate interpretation of murmuration, we would certainly see something more akin to a mob scene, every bird for him- or herself. But midair collisions are rare despite there being thousands of birds flying within fractions of inches of one another at speeds up to 20 mph.

Mathematicians seem to be closer to decoding murmuration from an Enough standpoint. Their current equations confirm that each starling's movements are influenced by every other starling regardless of the size of the flock and regardless of the position of each bird in the flock. The closest equations they find to explain murmuration come from the science of the criticality of crystal formations—systems poised on the brink that are "capable of near-instantaneous transformation."

Did they say "near-instantaneous transformation"? It is obvious that the birds are "communicating" with one another midflight not by verbally or physically signaling one another, but through some other capacity of telepathic consciousness that involves the kind of instantaneous transfer of information we observe in the Zero Point Field. Transform!

You + the Vibrational

How do we move from the Share message of the geese to the Transform message of the starlings? How do we experience murmuration? The shift is simpler than we might think. It involves moving our perspective from the head to the heart.

We are so used to having to work hard to make things happen in our lives. With the head as the taskmaster, we assume it is necessary to order, weigh, strategize, and plan our way to what we want. When the need arises to involve others in our activities, we assume it is necessary to convince, win over, persuade, guide, direct, teach, and reward them so they will do what we need them to do to bring our plan to fruition. While all this effort is going on, we worry if everything will work out. We worry about the things we cannot directly control, and we experience stress when we perceive that no matter what we do, we cannot guarantee our desired outcome and a sense of security that the future will go our way. All of this activity is very effort-intensive, thought-intensive, and emotion-intensive. No wonder life often feels overwhelming and complicated! What if this much striving and worrying is not a requirement for good things to happen? What if there was an easier and more effective way?

As stated earlier, the Never Enough Story has taught us since childhood that life is a series of transactions. If we want something, whether it is love, approval, a smile, a friend, or money, we think we need to earn it by complying with an external standard or protocol of some kind. As life goes on, we generalize this transactional perspective to encompass virtually everything we do, unconsciously apportioning to ourselves only what we believe is equal to our worthiness and effort. The underlying message is that we aren't inherently deserving of having what we want. We aren't enough as we are. With exceptions for exceedingly rare events like winning the lottery, we aren't lucky enough to get what we want without devoting a significant amount of blood, sweat, and tears and "paying our dues" to get it.

The transactional perspective is so pervasive in our culture that we tend to discount or ignore the many events that happen in our lives that could only be described as effortless. No payment or quid pro quo required. These are events like receiving a premonition that prevented something bad from happening or that caused you to be in the right place at the right time for something good to happen. What about the miracle of love at first sight, a brilliant solution that just pops into your head, the total bliss experienced in meditation or when sitting peacefully in nature, a dream which points you in the right direction, a chance meeting that changes your life? We all have these experiences that come to us when we are not thinking or in any way willing them into being. Life happens. Some people seem to have many more of these grace-full experiences than others. Why is that? And is it possible to receive more of these gifts of grace in our own lives? Yes, I believe it is.

Knowing that good things come to us in two ways—through striving or through grace, it may not occur to us that in every moment we are choosing (mostly unconsciously) between the two. We choose when we perceive life primarily through either our head or our heart. When we trust, when we let go of a need to control the outcome, when we dwell in the moment with a peaceful, relaxed expectation that good will come to us at the right time because we are enough, we are opening the door for grace to come in. When we distrust grace and don't feel that we are deserving of it, when we either define our prospects by our past experiences or become preoccupied with future goals, the door to grace closes to us. Possibilities collapse into a transactional, mechanical, linear arrangement where the rule is "input equals output." We have been taught to live this way most of our lives. It is when our guard is down and we revert to our baseline state that we restore our natural pathway to grace.

When you are exerting control, you are not energetically open to grace. The universe is trying to make a delivery to you, but no one is home to sign for the package. When you are engaged in striving, you are actually doing things the slow, hard way. Because you only expect to receive through a transactional relationship between input and output, you are collapsing the field of possibilities for how you can receive what you want, from whom, and where. Grace doesn't comply with a narrow set of rules. It often arrives from the places you least expect and in a form or manner that surprises you. When you put your intention out into the universe, it is important therefore to add "This or something better, from any source, both expected and unexpected, in right timing and for my highest good." Not only does this place you in receiving mode, but it allows you to receive miracles and vastly expands the avenues to fulfilling your dreams.

You will notice that striving resembles most closely the masculine or yang paradigm. The idea that we must be independent, self-sufficient, hardworking, action-oriented, impressive, unswerving, and exert our ideas and our muscle in order to achieve what we want is, we've been taught, the surest way to success, the proverbial "self-made man." And yes, this model has contributed and achieved much. I'm not trying to diminish it in any way, nor am I promoting the idea that we can have everything we want with no effort at all. What I am saying is that there is a time and place for genuine effort; but when we make no room in our process for partnering with grace, when we hold the reins too tightly with the rational, linear mind, we make things vastly more difficult for ourselves. Without the mechanics of receiving and allowing (the feminine/yin), we neglect to employ the most powerful forces the universe has to offer as our partner: grace.

Moving from the Head to the Heart

My interpretation is that humanity was not designed to be dominated by the head. There is evidence from both indigenous wisdom and modern science that it is the heart that should have natural dominion over the head. The Aztecs predicted a "great movement" on Earth at about this time, which I interpret as the movement from the head to the heart. Near the Four Corners, where Utah, Colorado, Arizona, and New Mexico meet, is a Hopi relic called Prophecy Rock. It tells of humanity's two paths. One path is the indigenous way, living connected to the body and the land and being guided by the heart. The other path is that of modern humanity, a state they represent as the head disconnected from the body and the body disconnected from Earth. The hieroglyph shows the two paths running parallel for some time, then one path veers sharply away from the other, representing what Gregg Braden refers to as a "choice point" for humanity. The path representing modern man depicts figures whose heads are disconnected from their bodies. This path abruptly stops, and only the indigenous path, whose figures are whole, goes on. Clearly, the prophecy is that intellect without connection to the heart, the body, and Earth is not sustainable.

In the 1970s, John and Beatrice Lacey, physiologists from the Fels Research Institute, found that the heart is much more than a blood-pumping organ. The heart is similar to the brain in that it emits an electromagnetic field. Electromagnetic fields store and exchange information. They showed that the electromagnetic field of the heart is five thousand times stronger than that of the brain. It has been measured to extend at least ten feet out from the body. (Ten feet is the current limit of the measuring device, not an indication of the outer boundaries of the field itself.) We know that the heart is exhibiting some kind of very powerful intelligence, one that by many orders of magnitude trumps that of the brain. This gives new meaning to the phrase, "The heart wants what the heart wants." The heart not only has wants of its own, it is by far the strongest personal transmitter and receiver of information and energy that we have.

So if the heart possesses some kind of intelligence, how is this intelligence different from the brain's intelligence? When we consider the role of the brain, its literal function is to sort, interpret, and store data. Its main function, then, is to take the whole of what we observe as our environment and our bodily sensations in that environment and break that down into parts for analysis, grouping, and comparison. The brain imposes interpretation, order, and bias on the world. The net effect is to eliminate novelty, reinforcing old patterns and limiting both what we see and what we expect to see. Data that doesn't fit our expectations must be rejected, discounted, reasoned away, or categorized as threats. The brain's main accomplishment is to help us to feel safe and in control. It is not, as we may have assumed, to present us with an accurate view of reality.

The heart, on the other hand, is not a dividing but a connecting organ. It, along with the circulatory system, provides life-giving nutrition to every cell without discrimination, replenishing the oxygen supply and delivering healing capacity anywhere it may be needed. Its main role, literal or symbolic, is to nourish, to connect, to make whole and healthy again. We also know our heart as the source of love and compassion, the place where a "tug at the heart" lets us know how connected we are. It is the place from which we pray and from where we send out our healing, nourishing prayers for peace and healing for the world.

The brain is perfectly suited to serve the Never Enough culture. The heart has been held tightly in check by the head. It is generally assumed that the head is the superior judge and that the heart is often foolish, whimsical, and unwise. There are so many places the heart is not welcome or consulted—in the workplace, in the classroom, on the battlefield, in the boardroom. In the Never Enough culture, the rational mind is generally considered the ultimate arbiter of truth, and physical evidence is the only valid proof. But when we look at how we actually make decisions, is this assumption even remotely accurate?

To most people, "heart intelligence" is not a common term. And yet, we've all experienced times when we have allowed something other than our rational mind the ultimate authority over our decisions. We are familiar with hunches, intuition, gut reactions, a sinking feeling, love at first sight, and feeling lucky. Intelligence that arrives as a feeling sense, a holistic "knowing," rather than a weighed calculation or logical accounting, is heart intelligence. Chances are, for the biggest and most complex decisions of our lives, such as whom to marry, where to live, which job to accept, we relied heavily on our heart intelligence. Where do these knowings about what is best for us come from? If our minds are tuned in to stimuli from our material environment, what or where is our heart tuned in to?

Consider the example of choosing an apartment. The head would be concerned with logistical and safety data: Can I afford the rent? Does it have the number of bedrooms and bathrooms I require? Will my commute be easy? Is it well maintained? Will the neighbors be noisy? The heart, on the other hand, is concerned with a feeling sense of connection: Can I see myself here? Does it feel like me? Is it my taste? Do I fit in with the neighbors? The heart is tuned to a sense of relationship between self and the physical environment, and to other subtle data that delivers a holistic sense of "fit." Much of this data cannot be seen or proven, only objectively felt.

Quantum physicists would tell you there is no such thing as purely objective data—that the very act of observation has an effect on what we are observing. We live in a dynamic, interconnected universe. This and countless other "strange forces at a distance" are what quantum physics have verified for over 115 years. It would not be a stretch to say that quantum physics could be the study of the "heart intelligence" present in the entire universe. It is intelligence that operates by a different set of laws than the universe we can see with the naked eye, yet it interpenetrates everything at a subtle, energetic level. These quantum forces are what our hearts are tuned in to, the soul's language that speaks as knowings, intuition, personal preferences, heart callings, and visions. Some call it the collective consciousness, the Akashic records, the morphogenetic field. It is why prayer creates healing even when the patient is at a distance and unaware he is being prayed for. It is what the HeartMath Institute calls "heart coherence," a state of inner peace and calm that vibrationally aligns our consciousness with that of Earth and each other so a line of heart-intelligent two-way communion is opened.

When the head is in charge, we suffer a kind of perceptual blindness that Eckhart Tolle refers to as "object consciousness." Our belief is that we need to have this or that or we need to do this or that in order to feel the way we want to feel. This is actually the slow, long way around. If instead we focused our intention directly on how we want to feel, we remove the interim steps of having to gain those feelings through objects or people or experiences beyond our direct control. We open up the possibilities for how these wonderful feelings will arrive in our lives, and we release unnecessary attachment to owning, controlling, or collecting objects—or people. Through heart awareness, we can focus on how we wish to feel, whether it is contentment, peace, relaxation, security, or love. Through a belief in Enough, we realize the sources of these emotions are already in and all around us. It is just a matter of focusing our attention and intention. Instead of conjuring up complicated visions and plans, we go right to the heart of what we want most and do not need to manage, worry, plan, or implement our way there. This welcomes the smallest, most mundane everyday experiences to be the triggers for these wonderful feelings. Even an intimate encounter with a flower can be the source of profound joy, Tolle says.

What brain intelligence was for the Never Enough paradigm heart intelligence is for the Enough paradigm. As the Russian poet Boris Pasternak once advised, "What is laid down, ordered, factual, is never enough to embrace the whole truth: life always spills over the rim of every cup." Heart intelligence senses and embraces life as a whole system, welcoming the infinite creativity and intelligence of the natural universe to join with us, to be in the driver's seat for our own and the world's greatest good. I believe this is where human evolution is leading us, awakening our intuitive and telepathic capabilities, allowing us to directly feel our intimate interconnectedness with one another and with all life on our beautiful planet. When we join the field of unified Enoughness, we are naturally drawn to act and interact based on love, compassion, and the greater good. It is time to realize that the mechanical age ended a century ago. This is the quantum age, the age of Enough. The heart is the main story now.

Humanity is ready for the message of the starlings. We are literally collectively in the gap between the message of the geese—how to collaborate and be a cooperative community— and the message of the starlings—how to more gracefully flow as a collective whole. This will absolutely involve consciously cultivating heart intelligence.

The Hundredth Monkey Effect and the Morphogenetic Field

In a theory known as the hundredth monkey effect, when a new idea enters the field of collective awareness of a species and is shared among the group, eventually it is bound to hit a threshold point by which the idea becomes integrated as a species-wide leap of understanding (Transform). When this leap happens, it is an emergence of a capacity that the Newtonian perspective cannot explain. It is as if the idea started with the kind of localized properties you would expect of a quantum particle. To be passed from one person to the next, the idea would need to be talked about or written about. Then it would need to be considered and integrated by the intellect, a process that could take some time. That is Newtonian. The hundredth monkey phenomenon predicts that after enough people know about the idea, something amazing happens. The idea transforms from a material object (particle) to a vibration (a waveform). As a waveform, the idea disperses everywhere, exhibiting nonlocal properties. At that point, the idea can be transferred to others not by slow methods like practice and learning, but by instantaneous quantum means, appearing in what Rupert Sheldrake refers to as the morphogenetic field, or the collective consciousness for all to instantaneously *know*. When the new idea appears in the morphogenetic field, anyone could theoretically gain access to it and understand it instantly. Future generations would be born with an inherent understanding of it. An effortless tipping point happens in which the collective unconscious takes a quantum leap.

Could this capability be real? Astronaut Edgar Mitchell conducted telepathy experiments while orbiting hundreds of thousands of miles above Earth in Apollo 14. The experiment consisted of him generating random symbols and telepathically "beaming" his thoughts of them to a person on Earth who recorded the impressions he received. Their results confirmed that human telepathy operates independently of both time and space. In other words, it is quantum. Distance has no effect on how long a telepathic message takes to go from one person to another. There are no distortions in accuracy, either. It suggests that by focused intention, ideas can be plucked from the Zero Point Field from anywhere in the universe instantly!

Some aboriginal tribes utilize telepathy as a main form of communion not only with one another but also with other species, a process called remote viewing. Evolutionary biologist and futurist Elisabet Sahtouris notes,

Working with and learning from indigenous people in the Americas has made me well aware that such telepathic communion was commonplace in many indigenous cultures and possibly even universal in our deep human past. The book Amazon Beaming, *for example, reports the contemporary experience of National Geographic photographer Loren McIntyre with the Mayoruna people of the Amazon, from whom he learned such communion as it was practiced by the entire tribe.*

Whether it is demonstrated by flocks of birds or by schools of fish, the evidence of this form of quantum communion has been with us since the beginning of time. If starlings, fish, and our indigenous brothers and sisters can do it, does modern man have the capacity to do it as well? I believe so. But we must cultivate a belief and an intention that we can and we will. The Enough Story predicts a rapid and exponential acceleration in our inherent capacity to perceive from interconnectedness, a capability that New Age teacher Gary Zukav calls "multisensory perception" and Buddhist teacher Thich Nhat Hanh calls "Interbeing" but which we commonly witness in ourselves and others as intuition, instinct, hunches, and telepathy. As we start to consciously exercise these parts of ourselves that have been put aside by the Never Enough Story, we will find that they come naturally and rapidly back to us. Then what we will find is that what the starlings are doing is nothing unusual at all. It only looks like magic because we don't acknowledge the magic of our own intuitive capabilities, our natural ways of sensing into the subtle. This awareness is a prerequisite to tapping into the Enoughness that is there for all of us.

Not intentionally planning it as an experiment, I can confirm this dynamic from direct experience. When I committed to writing this book, I heard a very clear directive to stop reading the works of others. I heard to go within to my own connection with the morphogenetic field to draw out the information, and only after pouring it out on the page was I to return to outward research to back up what had been accessed directly. What I found was this: The same knowings, with the same words and images I have shared with you, have shown up in disparate places through people sharing their individual dreams, scientific findings, visions, journeys, poetry, and the like. The Enough work is not a synthesis of my own intellectual inquiry, but has been first and foremost a vibrational field that many are already tapping into. Imagine my excitement as I began to look for confirmation of Enough only to find it everywhere with little or no effort at all. What was confirmed was global human murmuration!

The most comforting message from the starlings just may be this: Unity consciousness is not only natural, but is completely compatible with individuality. In other words, the starlings don't cease to be individuals with autonomous needs, thoughts, lives, and free will. But they can choose to transcend their individuality at times, and when they do, what is created is something truly sublime, something that could not be achieved by an individual acting alone.

Could it be that the murmuration is confirming the human dynamics that could occur as we begin to play more deliberately in the Zero Point Field? Could it be that we ourselves are capable of mass "instantaneous transformation?" As we continue to struggle to solve our collective problems using mind-to-mind and ego-to-ego dynamics, perhaps we are being shown a way of greater speed, grace, and ease by the starlings, a new way of presencing ourselves in the Zero Point Field—*human* murmuration!

It's All One Story—An Enough Story

If you have been paying close attention to the pattern running throughout this chapter, perhaps you are noticing that there is a single theme that unites the domains of the natural, the subtle, the vibrational, and the interrelational. Quantum science, General Systems Theory, biomimicry, and starlings are all demonstrating *the exact same thing*: evidence of an Enough Story of unfathomable untapped abundance all around and within us! The pessimists and doomsayers may assume that it is too late to solve many of the world's most critical problems, but they are assuming that we are remaining locked in the Never Enough mindset, the .001 percent of human consciousness that is focused on the story of materiality (particle). It is hard to imagine that anything would remain unsolvable as we begin to play together in the 99.999 percent (the waveform)!

Recovering Our Hidden Enoughness

It is from these underexplored frontiers of the natural, the subtle, the vibrational, and the interrelational that we will naturally receive more than enough resources to bring about planetary transformation. These areas have been blind spots to the constricted Never Enough worldview. They represent the Enough miracles that no one sees coming. Not only are intelligence, creativity, and genius constantly streaming in from the collective unconscious, urging us forward, but as we recover our natural heart coherence with the ecosystems and communities in which we live, our solutions and inventions rapidly, gracefully take shape as holistic and compatible with the greater good every time. When that happens, we will be shocked at how bulky, time-consuming, complicated, and ineffective any process driven by a worldview of separate egos and competition once was. We will wonder why we waited so long to notice the intelligent abundance that was there all along.

I believe that the main mission of the Enough Message is to help us understand the shift that is already taking place all around and within us. The shift in paradigms does not need to happen this time through violent or painful revolution. We do not need to worry about convincing anyone or tearing any institution down brick by brick. That is the old Newtonian way, the Never Enough way of force. When we personally choose to engage with the old perspective, we cannot avoid experiencing or perpetuating the suffering. We now clearly have a choice.

Our Responsibility as Holons

You've probably heard the saying, "We don't see things as they are. We see things as *we* are." What this means is the person we need to engage in this transformation is ourselves—just ourselves. Quantum mechanics and the morphogenetic field will take care of the rest. As holons, what we do to advance as individuals always brings the hundredth monkey tipping point nearer. As long as we understand this, we will not engage in futile and energy-grabbing efforts to try to act as heroes battling the Never Enough Story. That story is wilting on the vine of its own accord. As we expand into new territories of consciousness and spiritual maturity, our forward-looking joy and irresistible aliveness act as magnets, drawing energy away from the Old Story without a fight.

It is important to be vigilant for the considerable traps of perception that will tell us that scarcity is growing on this planet and it is our job to stop it. If we stay focused on the Never Enough Story, it will seem as though the crises are getting much worse. The fear is growing in the Never Enough culture, and rightly so because the Old Story is dying.

What can we do? Turn off the TV. Unsubscribe from emails and unfriend any groups that perpetuate anger, fear, or hopelessness. Participate in sacred ceremonies and wisdom circles where you can safely purge your pain, disappointment, sadness, and rage and help to purge humanity's collective pain, disappointment, sadness, and rage. Shield yourself from anything or anyone who causes negativity to root or grow within you. Work on dissolving any patterns that tend to seduce you back into the old scripts—the dramas, obligations, codependence, martyrdom, and victimhood. You do not need to take in that fear or experience that pain a minute longer. Keep your perception expanded in alignment with the Enough world you *do* want. Notice and contribute love, beauty, connection, wisdom, gratitude, and belonging wherever you can. Find others with whom you share the resonance of the New Story.

Part Two

Using the Enough Message to Benefit Ourselves and the World

This section examines each sentence of the Enough Message separately, exploring how the process gracefully guides and supports us as we commit to living a new planetary story.

⊸ 5 ⊸

I Am Enough

*I am precious and unique. I am here to learn, create, and grow—
not because I am not already enough, but for the joy of experiencing
my inborn capacity to provide what the world needs.*

In 2013 alone, an estimated $55 billion was spent in the United States on psychotherapy and mood-altering drugs. This is a staggering amount for a society that is said to be the shining example of freedom and democracy, one that has supposedly been built by the collective voice of its people. These higher ideals are trumped every time by the long shadow of the Never Enough worldview. Never Enough always conflicts with our inner sense of well-being. We get the message early in life that there is a narrow formula by which we earn praise and attention, a formula for being accepted as being "good enough." If we stray from this formula, we are told, we risk rejection, loneliness, and marginalization.

But what happens when we follow the Never Enough cultural formula and bad things happen anyway? Many in the millennial generation, saddled with huge college tuition debt and no job prospects, are finding out, as are seniors who lost almost half of their savings in the 2008 stock market crash. Ask those in the military who have faithfully served our country, returning with broken bodies and broken spirits. We are discovering that the simple formula that we thought would guarantee our enoughness has failed us.

Those born before the 1970s remember a time when the world didn't feel nearly as insecure, unpredictable, scary, and out of control. The Never Enough Story seemed to work for a time, labeled as the American Dream. Gradually, however, we began noticing disturbing changes; an erosion in the ability of the Never Enough contract to deliver what it promised. And yet, when we respond by feeling depressed or hopeless, we are told to work on ourselves with therapy or to numb ourselves with antidepressants. I would suggest that instead of a sign of our collective weakness and inadequacy, these symptoms so common in the world today are humanity's collective "canary in the coal mine" response to a sick paradigm that is not capable of creating or supporting our health and well-being.

Let me be clear: If you are currently in therapy or taking prescription antidepressants, I am not advocating that you should stop. I am simply saying that the need for these interventions did not come from some inner deficit within you, but from a flawed cultural paradigm that is toxic and that infects us all to some degree. To break the cycle of infection, we need some means of separating ourselves from the illness-producing conditions that run rampant in the Never Enough paradigm.

This is more difficult to do than we might think because we have inadvertently internalized the paradigm. For example, if I were to ask you, "Are you enough?" what would you say? If you are like me, your response might be something like this: You'd do a quick scan of your failures and disappointments, weighing them against the successes, and likely say, "No, I'm not enough. Not yet anyway." Or you might say, "I'm a work in progress."

It is amazing how automatically we translate "Are you enough?" to "Have you done enough?" or "Do you have enough?" I didn't ask if you had achieved enough or if you owned enough. I asked if you *are* enough. This is an entirely different question. Expressions like "Are you man enough?" reveal how confused we are about the difference between who we *are* and what we *do* or *have*. You are already enough, and the Never Enough paradigm that has convinced you otherwise is a manmade myth. In this chapter, I'll share some strategies for gaining a direct, personal experience of your enoughness so you can know that it is true: You are enough.

What It Means to Be Enough

It may seem obvious, but to recover our sense of being enough, we first need to acknowledge our own beingness. In the Never Enough Story, there is no room for beingness. Since beingness cannot be measured, it does not fit the materialistic lens we use in this current era. The Never Enough Story therefore automatically substitutes something measurable—what we do or what we have—for what we are. Because we are what we do, we have to prove that we are enough over and over again. Can you see how exhausting this is and how it keeps us on a perpetual treadmill of *doing*? In essence, we are convinced that we must purchase our sense of selfhood. This is not true identity. This is not true beingness. A newborn child has not achieved anything and does not own anything, but would you say he or she is not enough? Is he or she worthy of being born? How about you? Are you enough? Are you worthy of being here on Earth? Well, of course you are. You are here, aren't you? When and how did you lose your enoughness?

To explain how I know on a very deep level that you are enough, I invite you to widen the lens from the manmade Never Enough Story to the biggest possible story we could use to explain reality, which is the story of the universe in its entirety. From the universe's perspective, every one of us is enough and has always been enough. We are part of a whole that is inseparable, complete, perfect, wondrous, and evolving. There are no mistakes or misfits. To deny any one of us is to deny the universe's wholeness. Every aspect of creation has a place in the whole that informs and serves the rest. Therefore, we were each born enough. The Never Enough Story does not want you to know that. It needs you to give your power away. It needs you to be unsure of yourself. It counts on you to believe you need to pay ever-increasing rent for the privilege of being alive. It counts on you to consume more than you really need because that keeps the Never Enough economy going.

Throughout this book I've asked you to join me in widening your lens of perception. I will be asking you to honestly assess if the Never Enough lens is the truth, and if you feel it is serving you, most of humanity, and the planet to your satisfaction. I believe we each know the truth. Our bodies and hearts know what we and the world need to be whole and healthy. Our confusion, disappointment, and frustration are not indications of our inadequacy; they are indications of our genius: our spirit's natural, healthy response to when our body and heart are screaming to be heard, but we do not feel we have the permission or the courage to follow their advice.

When I speak of "widening the lens," I am also referring to increasing our depth perception. What do I mean by this? I mean noticing the depths of who you are as a multisensory being who can connect directly to your sense of place in the vast cosmos and know you are in harmony with all the other parts. I mean giving yourself permission to listen to what your body and your heart are trying to tell you.

Since we have been subjected to the Never Enough Story for so many millennia, it is understandable that it will feel strange and maybe even scary to move beyond the assumption of scarcity, but the abundance beyond the Never Enough Story has always been there and always will be. It is not going away. Nothing and no one can sever the connection we have with this deeper territory, though we can be made to forget to access it.

Why the Enough Message Is So Elusive

How do we transition from "I am not enough" to "I am enough" in practical, personal terms? What hastens the leap of perception within us? Ultimately, it must come down to the aha moment when we choose to believe we are enough, really enough.

What follows are some doorways to reclaiming "I am enough."

- Feeling belongingness instead of accumulating belongings

- Appreciating our unique and precious gifts

- Realizing we are part of a universal meta-trend

- Valuing feminine roles and qualities

- Taking our power back from experts

The Never Enough belief system created the spiritually bereft mechanical and industrial ages. The Never Enough mantra is that we are what we do. The message is that we are what we have. There is no value or greater meaning to us beyond that. This cultural value system treats nature as well as people as objects, valuable only for what they can do or provide that can be monetized. When we objectify someone or something, we must deny their sacredness and their irreplaceable preciousness. We must deny the unseen depths of the entire world, reducing it to a machine that produces material wealth. So much of the wealth the Never Enough economy claims to produce is actually wealth derived from nature's bounty and at the expense of exploited workers who remain faceless and nameless to the consumer. It is my hope that when we see how universal the devastating reach of the Never Enough economy has been, then we will forgive ourselves for participating in it, will begin healing from it, and will collectively create new ways to divest ourselves from it.

With more evolved perception, we can reclaim our depths and align ourselves with our true nature, which is also the true nature of the universe. I will share many stories in chapter 8 that the shift to an Enough economy is already well under way. We were not created to be blind consumers or exploiters. We were not created to compartmentalize and repress our love and compassion. We are clearly worthy of rejoining nature's enduring story of Enough as partners, advocates, and co-creators. We now have a choice for how to "be" in the world, a way that feels infinitely right in our bones, a way with deep, satiating meaning.

Appreciating Our Essence

I was recently at a neighborhood party speaking with a friend who is an outstandingly gifted designer and craftsman. He asked me to explain my Enough perspective. After I explained it, he replied, "So how do I feel enough when there is so much out there left to achieve and want? I don't see how I can ever feel enough unless I pretended that the things I still want do not exist." I couldn't provide an immediate answer, and it bothered me all night, as the question was earnest and sincere. I needed to unpack why I don't perceive achievements or things as the rock-solid imperative that my friend and most people seem to feel it is. I don't think the issue is whether material things tempt us. I think the key is having a conscious awareness of our precious beingness. Beingness is not visible in the way a new car, a promotion, or the latest gadget is; but beingness can bolster and satiate like none of those other things.

If I were to answer my friend now, I would begin with a series of questions. "Who are you in that moment when you are totally and happily engaged in the creative process of designing a beautiful piece of furniture or a custom home? Who are you as a recipient of inspired ideas, as a translator of those ideas onto paper and into wood and glass? Can you feel how you are enough in every way? Can you stand in awe of what flows through you when you are creating these beautiful things?"

If we were to reflect on our most contented moments, we would find that they arise from directly experiencing our beingness. We lose track of time. We exist in those moments in a kind of engaged bliss and aliveness. We are in alignment with divine inspiration and flow. We are in service to what the world needs. We aren't just creating things like robots in order to buy other things. We are creating as a pure expression of who we are. We are in the quantum field of aliveness.

One way to access the feeling of "I am enough" is to find some kind of working language to describe beingness so we can share, engage, and relate to it more consciously. So we can know that it is real. So we can spend time with it. So we can share what we know about it.

Early in my spiritual quest, I heard a lecture by Deepak Chopra about the inner observer who steps back and simply notices what we are doing and thinking without judgment. We are doers and thinkers, but the observer is also us. The observer is unchanged by outer circumstances, and therefore is the most enduring, the most permanent aspect of the self, our core essence. On the level of essence we are completely enough at all times. Does the observer need a promotion, a new car, or the latest gadget to be enough? No. Is the observer diminished when these outer markers are out of reach? No. The observer is always even, always enough. Practicing observer-mind as often as we can is an important practice in realizing our enoughness.

Whether or not we have a working language to talk about essence, it is absolutely a natural human ability to have a direct experience of it. Essence is the heart of who we are, our most pure state of being. The broken promise of the industrial and digital ages was to give us more leisure time for personal pursuits. This should have led to more time to reawaken to our essence selves, but instead we have been encouraged to fill our free time with the kinds of diversions and addictions that take us even farther away from our essence. We have been encouraged to work longer and harder to obtain more things. How do we resist these outward temptations that offer instant gratification but do not really satisfy or last?

I believe one possible answer is to not only create a regular practice of sitting quietly somewhere to be with our beingness but also to bring that powerful, tangible spacious awareness into whatever we do or wish to do, think about or wish to think about. It is so difficult to resist the habit of filling every minute with activity. But if we begin to observe how much better we feel when we create space for our beingness to speak to us, I believe we will easily collect the proof we need to commit to having more of it.

Recently, I was facilitating a visioning session for a group of people who had been business partners for several years but were experiencing some difficult disagreements. My session was designed to help them focus on making their core agreements with one another explicit. The intention was that by coming to an agreement about how they wanted to *be* as a group, this would lead to more clarity and alignment about what they wanted to *do* together.

We began with a guided visualization in which they were asked to envision working in an ideal group that reflected the core agreements they would like to have. How did it look and feel to them? One participant wrote a beautiful, heartfelt poem on the spot that moved everyone deeply. Another created a drawing that incorporated words like trust, truth, vulnerability, peace, and respect. In these moments, the feel of the room was connected, open, trusting, and peaceful. Moments later, I asked them to test a current work challenge against the new agreements they had shared. Very quickly, the old tapes started running. Anger, insults, blame, tears—the opposite of the agreements they had just expressed. Because our hearts had just moments earlier been wide open to one another, the sudden shift was jarring and painful. My point is this: Becoming a cohesive "we" is very hard work, and it is sacred work. It is challenging to erase old tapes and patterns, but it is my hope that having viscerally experienced the contrast between these two states of being back to back will cause us to ask, "What kind of world do I prefer? What ought to be? Which of these two realities allows flow to support our most precious intentions?"

We are a species coming to a perceptual tipping point. We are fed up with the inadequacy of the old model of position taking as well as "negotiation." Even when we give these two methods of relating a positive spin, both are rooted in an assumption of separation—your needs versus my needs. Our political and economic systems are based on separation, creating winners and losers. Something deeper wants to arise, a grounding in essence-to-essence connection, the finding of common ground, the ground Rumi pointed to when he wrote, "Out beyond the ideas of wrongdoing and rightdoing, there is a field. I'll meet you there." I believe we are capable of meeting in that field. The problem is not that we aren't capable or willing; the problem is that the Never Enough Story has been giving us the wrong directions for how to get there, and we have been faithful to those directions, still believing they will eventually lead us to the outcomes we desire. They don't. Almost every institution and structure on Earth today unconsciously operates from these faulty instructions, leading back to Never Enough. No wonder it often feels like we are driving in circles—*we are*!

Noticing Your Divine Gifts

Part of recovering a sense of your own enoughness is cultivating a greater appreciation for your divine gifts—not the marketable, exploitable skills and knowledge you have accumulated over the years, but "who you are" as a divine being with a meaningful purpose on Earth. Society values and rewards certain kinds of skills and knowledge, usually those that can be commoditized, but it is up to you to value your divine gifts and to notice how they affect the world for the better. It may well be that these gifts are things that you take for granted, have difficulty categorizing, or that would never bring you a paycheck. Your gifts may include compassion, fairness, integrity, patience, deep listening, the ability to make people feel calm, and a willingness to support those who are going through grief or transition. You notice things others do not. You anticipate outcomes long before others do. There are many divine gifts that we share with others every day.

To get in touch with your divine gifts, reflect on your inter-actions and the presence you feel called upon to bring to people or situations. How are your contributions different than or adding to what others bring? What are you attuned to that others are not? What is the quality of your presence? Perhaps think of it as a unique vibration, one that radiates something the world truly needs, such as peace or courageous vulnerability or forgiveness or love. In her book *My Stroke of Insight*, Dr. Jill Bolte Taylor, a brain scientist, shares her experience as a patient recovering from a massive stroke. In her altered state after the stroke, she was able to notice how much people's energy affected her healing process and instructed all her visitors and medical attendants to "take responsibility for the kind of energy they bring me." Faith, optimism, non-judgment; all these aid healing. Pity, worry, and fear do not.

It could be said that we radiate energy that affects those around us at every moment. What energy do you bring to people or situations? In what unseen ways might you be contributing to someone else's growth or healing? Sit with your divine gifts and see if you can put them into words or phrases. Make them visible to yourself in some way—write them down or create a collage or drawing that incorporates them. Then allow gratitude to flow through you for having volunteered to bring these divine gifts into the world. I assure you they are enough.

Clues in Science and Technology

Trends in science and technology always mirror where human consciousness is evolving. For example, the idea of the Internet or World Wide Web mirrors our growing conscious awareness of how interconnected we are with one another. What we see now is that science and technology are huddled at the Zero Point Field where subtle forces act in ways we would consider strange or miraculous. As stated in chapter 3, the readiness to acknowl-edge the subtle, or what lies beyond the obvious and tangible, is an evolutionary step in expanding our perception beyond the bounds of Never Enough. Quantum scientists and high tech innovators already know that scarcity is not the underlying dynamic of the world we live in. We live in a world that is completely underwritten by vast, rich, invisible abundance at the quantum and cosmic level. The average person cannot "see" the energy or information floating around in thin air, but they can confirm these strange forces every time they use data clouds, the Internet, Wi-Fi, solar panels, and scanning devices. We know that technologies can become dangerous when our consciousness does not evolve with them. Acknowledging the subtle is therefore both a personal and collective imperative for humankind. When we wake up to the deep value of the subtle within us and the bounty that it offers, we can relate to these technologies and respect their power and potential for good or ill. When we act from our essence instead of our egos, we are available to connect with others more authentically and responsibly. We are ready to acknowledge that the subtle is real and that everything is connected and interdependent. Our responsibility becomes greater rather than less when we acknowledge this fact.

Valuing Feminine Roles and Qualities

Recovering our connection to the universal Enough Story is greatly assisted by recovering the lost feminine qualities within ourselves. Because the Enough Story is assisted by the feminine, it is a very nurturing and healing process in which to engage. The feminine qualities allow, yield, let go, open up to the subtle within us and all around us. Feminine qualities are more receptive than assertive, more observing than judging, more organic than formulaic, more hearing than speaking, more interrelating than individuating. Nowhere are the feminine qualities more necessary than to clear the debris of the Never Enough paradigm, the deep loneliness and wounded self-perceptions we carry within us as "I am not enough."

The more concrete and visible qualities of the masculine, such as action, deductive reasoning, initiative, and physicality, have made up the backbone of the Never Enough civilization. We are well trained in these ways of acting and perceiving. This does not make the masculine a conspirator in Never Enough. It has rather been a servant to it. But anytime half of our collective capability is devalued or neglected, it creates an imbalance and a separation. It also means that without the feminine, we cannot achieve an accurate sense of the whole that we are, which creates perceptual error and suffering.

Evolution isn't always a pretty process. The pendulum swings back and forth between the extremes until we cultivate sufficient longing for wholeness and convergence, drawing us to complete the cycle of learning. The Never Enough Story has been one of those extreme pendulum swings, leaving many on the planet today deeply longing for wholeness, which requires us to utilize our feminine qualities. Qualities we long for such as kindness, patience, nurturance, deep listening, unconditional love, sharing, community, compassion, and peace are in scarce supply when the feminine is not adequately represented or valued. By cultivating an awareness of "the other half of our soul," we reclaim the missing piece we all need to achieve wholeness and to enter the wider Enough Story. This is healing. Therefore, it benefits all beings on Earth—both male and female—to consciously develop an awareness of and respect for the subtle feminine qualities within.

The Pilgrim, the Seer, and the Sovereign: Feminine Archetypes

How do men and women gain an appreciation for the value of the feminine aspects of their being? A couple of years ago, I heard an interview conducted by Feminine Power with author Lucia René. In that interview, Lucia spoke about three feminine roles: the Seer, the Sovereign, and the Soldier. I found it very

helpful to frame feminine qualities through these three archetypes, especially because two of the three—the Sovereign and
the Seer—are roles that are specifically attuned to the subtle. As
we make these roles more visible, we begin to notice and value
them as part of the wider spectrum of gifts we possess as human
beings. Doing so hastens the movement into an Enough culture.

The Soldier/Hero/Pilgrim

The Soldier   The Soldier archetype is the central figure of our
current Never Enough paradigm, one we refer to widely as the
Hero. The Soldier (Hero) has taken central stage in our society
and continues to dominate our culture through movies, television, and video games. As a parent of a teenage son, I have
been very concerned about the narrow formula of entertainment directed at teen boys. The story line always seems to be
the same. It could easily seem that there is no choice for a young
man other than to expect his life to unfold like a video game in
which he receives respect and rewards for killing and conquer-
ing but not for nurturing and listening.

The Hero   The Hero is the main figure we have used for millennia to pass down the Never Enough Story itself: stories of
conquest, war, technological "progress," dominion over nature,
and winning. It is important to note that the Hero role is not an
invention of the Never Enough Story. It, like the masculine, was
co-opted and stripped of its essence by the Never Enough paradigm. This is why I refer to our modern concepts of the Hero
as "the *Fallen* Soldier," a hero who is a mere shadow of himself
because he has been stripped of his heart by a paradigm that
needs him to not feel.

The Hero archetype is deeply embedded in the human
psyche. The desire to forge new paths and to be bold to protect
what and whom we love is natural, but only when it is connected to the heart and in service to the whole, which includes

the feminine. The image of the Hero that we have adopted is one whose anger and rage are legitimized, whose ego is exalted, and whose brutality is excused as bravery. Somehow the enemy is never perceived to be as human as the ally or as justified in his hatred and brutality as the Hero. In reality another culture's heroes and our culture's heroes are motivated by the same thing—a desire to serve their country. Therefore, the Hero story we are used to telling is not one of ultimate truth, but one of false distortion. It is one of separation, not of wholeness.

Heroes have been put in the unenviable position of doing the dirty work for a paradigm ripe with hatred, prejudice, and greed. When the Hero is instead put to work in service to the sacredness and interrelatedness of life, he is available to defend life and peace. He is available to stand up for what his heart and body know support the well-being of all. We also may know the Hero as an activist, a charismatic leader, a CEO, an inventor or scientist. It is his willingness to boldly assert himself that is at the heart of this archetype, not his willingness to go to war. The most powerful Hero is one who is led by his heart to stand up for a beautiful vision for what ought to be and for what could be, someone like Mahatma Gandhi, the Dalai Lama, or Martin Luther King, Jr. Though the Hero may be most comfortable taking the lead, a true hero knows that he is not superior to others, nor does he act independently. He serves wholeness, which includes Lucia's other roles – the Seer and Sovereign.

Below, I've adapted and expanded Lucia's Seer, Sovereign, Soldier model, drawing upon my experiences working in women's circles for many years. I have framed the three archetypes in terms of their potential to establish and support the arising Enough culture. One adaptation I have made is to change the Soldier to a Pilgrim. The founder of Schumacher College, Satish Kumar, has spoken passionately and eloquently about the Pilgrim. His inspired vision of a Pilgrim instead of a Hero better reflects the peaceful, connected, and forward-looking qualities that will be called for in the shift while still retaining the sense of leadership and boldness I believe Lucia's Soldier role embodies. Presenting all three roles as feminine is to call further attention to this less traveled territory in our collective psyche, though all three could be considered gender-neutral.

The Pilgrim   The Pilgrim is the role most intimately engaged with the old Never Enough paradigm, challenging its assumptions, pointing out illusions, contrasting what is with what could be. The Pilgrim serves in the roles of activist, whistleblower, and change agent. The Pilgrim exhibits courage and initiative in her willingness to challenge the status quo and to help innovation move ahead in bold but practical ways. The Pilgrim leads by nudging old systems through truth telling, influencing, lobbying, gathering resources, and drawing attention to opportunities for improvement. When we look at change efforts, very often there is one or more Pilgrim figure present, someone who can rouse passion and action.

Hooks That Hold Back the Pilgrim   If the Pilgrim is rooted in old Never Enough principles, she may get caught up in anger and indignation. She may feel a need to blame or shame the old power structure into changing, increasing the mood of separation and violent revolution. But blame and shame can never get us to the Enough world we are hoping to create.

She will need to be vigilant for the old ideas and words of separation, and orient people toward embracing a more unifying and empowering way forward, using her charisma as a magnet for the new ideas and ways of Enough. She will also need to avoid spending too much time trying to fix symptoms of existing systems, as the battle can be long and trying when one gets mired in the vibration of the old.

Remaining humble and collaborative are also challenges for a Pilgrim, for she is a natural-born leader. The old hierarchical and individualistic roles will seem to fit. So she will need to work to resist these learned archetypal patterns, instead stepping into roles as facilitator and coach, helping people to share leadership and decision making with her. The Pilgrim's charge is to steward the big picture by seeing the work that needs to be done to get the ball rolling in a new direction.

Being a Pilgrim requires one to wield personal power and initiative, and this is why Pilgrims often have extroverted, charismatic, self-confident, and articulate personalities. Pilgrims are risk-takers and do not shy away from what is difficult, new, or scary. As such, a Pilgrim deals with her own failures and mistakes well, seeing them as the price of admission to learning a new and better way forward. Those at the front lines of a movement tend to be Pilgrims. Their tools are words, people skills, hard work, and a sharp intellect. Pilgrims are absolutely essential on the evolving edge between paradigms to help people break free of old systems and coalesce energy for building the new.

How the Pilgrim Needs the Seer and the Sovereign   The risk to pilgriming work is that it is intense and can lead to burnout and feelings of isolation and loneliness. When conflict with the old ways arises, it can also be dangerous. When a movement is coalesced by a magnetic personality, it can become overly dependent on the individual. This can be quite a heavy burden and a constant demand on the Pilgrim, making it difficult to obtain a sense of balance between one's personal life and professional life. This is where the Sovereign and the Seer can help anchor and replenish the Pilgrim, and the Seer can help the Pilgrim to discern what opportunities are most likely to offer a worthy return for the effort.

The Seer

The Seer has much to offer to bring the spiritual insight human-ity needs to trust the upcoming shift. The vision she possesses allows others to take leaps of faith, to trust their own intuitive capacities, and to follow their hearts. She is also a key advisor, sensing the motives, integrity, and agendas of those she tunes into. She will intuitively know who is telling the truth, who is trustworthy, and whose heart is open. In this way, she can help others to avoid missteps such as investing in people or projects that are unlikely to bear fruit.

The Seer is in touch with the subtle forces of energy and vibration that guide and shape all of life. Often she sees, hears, or senses what others cannot, in touch with subtle realms of energy, vibration, and spirit and receiving her prompts from the morphogenetic field. The Seer may be clairvoyant, clairaudient, or simply tuned in to a subtle yet powerful form of guidance. The Seer brings the subtle to the surface to be considered. She brings understanding of the connectedness underlying all things and guiding all things. The Seer is a natural systems thinker. She is able to tap into the morphogenetic field to sense where the future is heading before others are aware. No one could deny that intuition and right timing are absolutely essential to any form of occupation, separating those who are able to capitalize on trends and upswings at precisely the right time from those who cannot. These are capabilities of the Seer.

Many Seers tend to go into esoteric fields, becoming counsel-ors, mystics, spiritual guides, psychics, shamans, healers, energy workers, and astrologers. Others quietly apply their visions, not calling attention to their source. Many Eastern, ancient, and indigenous cultures hold a place of great reverence and honor for the shamans, oracles, and wisdom keepers. In Western society, while we greatly downplay the role of Seers as social change agents who possess valuable and accurate information, a significant number of us do seem to seek them and their spiritual advice for our own personal counsel.

Intuition is an inherent human capacity of which the ancients were well aware, but we are just now giving ourselves permission to foster this gift in a public way in the West. There is a steady acceleration in the number of people who are accessing these capacities with ever greater acuity through mindfulness practices of all kinds. So many, in fact, that it seems we are headed for a hundredth monkey tipping point where multisensory/extrasensory capacity will eventually become widely accepted as simply "our human nature." As we notice and consciously work with our multisensory capacities, we find that there are vast amounts of information to be accessed beyond the five senses and the logical, linear mind.

As discussed earlier, scientific evidence confirms extrasensory perception in the animal kingdom, including humans. Whether it is murmuration, a dog knowing when its owner is coming home, or human remote viewing experiments, it is becoming more obvious that the Never Enough culture has systematically downplayed what is a naturally occurring capacity in the entire animal kingdom. With a reasonable amount of effort, this capacity can be recovered and honed by any of us in service to our evolving consciousness.

Hooks That Hold Back the Seer   Collectively, as we wake up to what is, we will also come face-to-face with the lies embedded in our current paradigm. When we realize how we have been misled by the powers that be, we will need time to process what understandably arises as anger, grief, and disappointment. This is a delicate time that calls upon the strength and comfort of the Sovereign, lest the Seer becomes angry, depressed, or disillusioned by the truth she is seeing.

As we step forward to see what is really there, we become powerful advocates for the truth. In many ways, the recent flurry of banking, spying, government, sports, and sex scandals indicates that our ability to accept the truth as a collective culture is vastly expanding. Our eyes are opening up. These incidents prepare us for the inevitable tidal wave of disclosures as the breakdown of the Never Enough paradigm continues to reveal illusions one by one. These "peeks behind the curtain" ask us to consider the most productive response and to hold the vision of a world in which love unites, consoles, and supports each and every one of us. When the Seer glimpses the enormity of humanity's ability to be multisensory co-creators, and the Pilgrim stands by her with solid strength and courage, the Seer, "the one who sees," becomes an incredibly inspiring and trusted catalyst for the liberation of humanity.

How the Seer Needs the Pilgrim and the Sovereign The Seer taps her potential by tuning out the cultural chatter in order to tune in to the quiet whispers of the subtle. This takes discipline and attention. The more the Seer is able to let go of emotional attachments to current situations, belief systems, and constraints, the farther and more clearly she will be able to "see." Her work depends on her ability to remove herself physically and emotionally from outside distractions so she can sense these subtle knowings without prejudice. Her sight is clearest when she focuses her consciousness through mindfulness. The Sovereign can hold a place for the Seer to experience peaceful contemplation and to grieve and dispel negative emotions, while the Pilgrim can take on the social and outer work that needs to be done and encourage a positive, steady, forward-thinking focus.

Truth Must Be at the Center If humanity as a species is moving toward developing greater intuitive capacities, this can only mean one thing: Truth must be at the center of anything we would build for the future. For if we are all moving in the direction of becoming multisensory seers, the Never Enough stories, illusions, and cover-ups will become ineffectual. The truth will simply be known by all. While we will at first feel vulnerable to be so exposed to one another, we will actually be able to relax into a simpler reality, for the presence of the false self is always a heavy burden to bear and steals energy and attention from our real work.

The Sovereign

The Sovereign is the archetype for which the least has been understood and appreciated. It is easy to pass over the role of the Sovereign, which, like the Seer, is working with the subtle and is therefore behind the scenes. While the Seer brings truth, the Sovereign anchors that truth in unconditional love and peace. She does this through her ability to *ground* and to *hold a field of nurturance and purity of intention.*

At the heart of the Sovereign is the nurturer, the tender of the home flame, the heart. Not since Roman times has the role of the Sovereign been venerated in an official way, other than as a divine ideal on a pedestal, but never as a human role worthy of societal position. It has since then been considered part and parcel with the role of mother, and therefore has been taken for granted by all our economic, political, and social systems. Sovereigns are often most comfortable in the role of supporting others as wives, mothers, friends, caregivers, and daughters. But we could go as far as to say that our society could not exist without the assumption of free labor from Sovereigns to care for children, the elderly, and the infirm. And because it is assumed that the Sovereign's labor is selflessly motivated, her services have been exploited by our culture for a very long time, feeding sexism and all sorts of gender inequalities. As such, there has been no outward incentive for men to cultivate their Sovereign nature.

As a group, women tend to internalize this treatment and have lower self-esteem than their male counterparts (I'm not Enough). The modern feminist movement has tried to address this self-esteem issue, but unfortunately it has not gone about it by elevating the Sovereign role but rather by encouraging Sovereigns to mold themselves into workers for the Never Enough machine. Even as recently as the Lean In campaign, we are still sending the message to young women to be more like the men of the corporation rather than asking corporations to learn from feminine sensibilities to respond more compassionately and holistically to the needs of workers, families, and communities. The purity of the desire to nurture and care for others is one of humanity's greatest and highest virtues. It is essential to building trust, mutuality and the well-being of mankind and the planet. It should not be exploited, but exalted.

We tend to equate the term "sovereign" with royalty. This conjures an image of a queen or king who rules over others. This is a misinterpretation of the Sovereign archetype, for the Sovereign is not aligned with "power over" but with "power with." In the feminine aspect, the Sovereign is one who holds a venerated place not by force, lineage, or physical authority, but by serving others, inviting and anchoring a sense of community, and practicing spiritual responsibility through the divine qualities of integrity, compassion, and purity of intention. She is the calm at the center of the storm, the rock solid foundation that brings a sense of safety and warmth to any group of which she is a part. Her purpose is to bring peace and nourishment to the parched human soul, a space to rest and rejuvenate. She stands steady, presiding over a space where deep healing can take place, where layers of the false self can be shed and the authentic self-expressed. Her power within is a protective force field that embraces humanity and all living beings as beloved family.

The ultimate representative of the Sovereign is our planet, Gaia herself. Gaia provides all that nurtures life—even the raw materials that make up our bodies. The ultimate reflection of how we treat the Sovereign in our society is how we treat Earth. We make demands on her that vary from dependence to entitlement to ownership. We take for granted that she can give endlessly, so we do not tend to take responsibility for helping to replenish her until she breaks down. When we learn that our survival is dependent on the Sovereign, we will understand the importance of the principle of reciprocity—we complete the cycle of abundance only when we include giving back to the Sovereign.

The Sovereign and the Sacred The Romans believed the Vestal Virgins performed an invaluable spiritual service for the empire, symbolized by the tending of the eternal flame. They realized that it was through the feminine Sovereign that gifts of nurturance and spiritual protection were bestowed upon the people. Without this sacred fire, it was feared that the collective human spirit could be snuffed out. If we were to compare our current society with a tribe in prehistory that honored the goddess, which revered the Sovereign, we would find that we have almost completely lost the sense of the sacred in daily life. The eternal flame is dim indeed. Rather than sourcing the sacred from the human spirit itself, we have invented various "cardboard cutout" substitutes—a plethora of benchmarks, musthaves, and status symbols that drive our rampant consumerism and encourage a sense of competition and superiority. None of these ephemeral forms are capable of feeding our hunger for deep sacred meaning and purpose.

Meaning is not a luxury. Humans require meaning in order to be in a state of well-being. But when the sense of the sacred is forgotten, everything in our world is reduced to being a means to an end, an object—even people. All is stripped of sacred meaning. We objectify ourselves when we see ourselves as something to be doled out to fulfill responsibilities and roles. When we give out of guilt, obligation, habit, or martyrdom, we have lost the replenishing source of our generosity just as surely as the fallen hero has lost the guiding compass that is his heart.

In our current time, we have strayed farther from the Sovereign's comforting gaze than we have in all of recorded history. Many women have had to cut themselves off from their own sacred Sovereign, believing other pursuits to be more lucrative and necessary to the status and security of themselves and their families. The result is a spiritually parched and distressed humanity. Perhaps one of the most healing actions we can take in service to humanity, then, is to elevate the Sovereign. We must recognize in ourselves the valuable service we perform whenever we fully engage in nurturing. We must glimpse again our own sacredness and the sacredness of all life. The rise of the feminine is an absolute requirement as we shift into Enough and complete our species-wide journey into wholeness.

The Hooks That Hold Back the Sovereign   The other meaning of sovereign is "whole unto itself." This is precisely how the Sovereign can best serve at this time, to become grounded and whole so she can bring her steadiness to humanity during stressful and changeful times. We have been used to seeing the disempowered, unhealed Sovereign, one who martyrs herself in service to others and then feels small, unseen and depleted as a result.

What we are asked to do now is to stand *within* the love we provide to others, and to see ourselves as the first recipient of that love. Self-love becomes the essential key to loving others well. This is what we mean by discovering our own inherent enoughness. We are willing to say no when it respects our well-being to do so. We see ourselves as worthy of our own self-care. We do it because we recognize how important it is to the world to have strong and healthy Sovereigns among us who are in their fullest health and vitality to serve others. We do it because we accept that we are enough to be worthy of respect and care.

In many ways, the path toward greater individual sovereignty is humanity's collective next step. Can we unplug from external structures, expectations, and norms; can we become less attached to the material world, all in service to becoming a community of whole and sovereign beings? Who better than the experienced Sovereigns on this Earth to lead others in this journey by sharing their expertise?

How the Sovereign Needs the Pilgrim and the Seer   Without the outward-acting finesse and courage of the Pilgrim and the multisensory confidence of the Seer, the gifts of the Sovereign may go unexpressed and unnoticed in the larger world. Clearly, the three in tandem are necessary for the new paradigm to break through as a brilliant, concentrated beam of light in the consciousness of humanity.

Honoring Ourselves as Integral to the Whole

The roles of the Pilgrim, the Seer, and the Sovereign are imperative to the unfolding Enough Story. Each role embodies a higher order capacity to attune to the untapped potential of subtle realms, bringing us enough abundance and creativity to manage the planetary shift with grace. As we look to these roles, we may recognize our own natural capacities in one or more of them. It is important to remember that we don't need to master all three in order to be enough as a planetary change agent. We can find these qualities in helpmates, colleagues, and friends and together be whole and strong.

As we press beyond old learned limitations, we may also find we are drawn to stretch ourselves into one or more of the roles that come less naturally to us. Sometimes we attract people with complementary qualities so we can learn how to grow into that part of ourselves more fully. If we have been quiet and contemplative, we may find we are willing to be more vocal and assertive. If we have taken on a leadership role our whole lives, we may find we have an urge to step back and to go within. When we settle into our own enoughness, we can follow these inner prompts to try something new. We can let go of any fear that we must do anything better than anyone else. There are no external benchmarks for being most authentically who we are. We just need to do our part by following our hearts moment to moment. Our gifts are enough. We are enough to make the right difference.

Pilgrim

Strengths: Courageous, confident, resourceful, active, knowledgeable

Tools: Passion, charisma, voice, action, strategy, intelligence

Needs: Renewal, trustworthiness companionability, nurturing, grounding, whole systems perspective

Seer

Strengths: Insightful, whole systems thinker, truth identifier, visionary, mystic, intuitive

Tools: Intuition, attunement, ritual, meditation, alchemy, right brain activities (art, dance, etc.)

Needs: Grounding, activity, practicality, nurturing, protection

Sovereign

Strengths: Healing, community cultivator, peaceful, flexible, senses others' needs, engenders trust, grounded

Tools: Love, listening, patience, nurturance, gentleness, healing modalities, responsiveness, body wisdom and natural cycles

Needs: Confidence, courage, recognition, voice, protection

The Crone

Author of *Women Who Run With the Wolves*, Clarissa Pinkola Estés, coined the phrase "dangerous old woman." I love the irony of the phrase, and I love that as a woman in my fifties, I am growing into one of them. Estés explains that postmenopausal women are the most dangerous people in the world to the status quo because at this stage of life, they are done people pleasing, done with needing male attention and approval, and have more time on their hands. They know who they are and what they want. In other words, they are virtually incorruptible.

I've regularly witnessed this power and wisdom in older women. We may joke and say that Grandma has become less agreeable, has lost her filter, or no longer cares what others think of her, but beneath this is a kind of awe and perhaps some envy at the degree of freedom she allows herself. How could it be that such a frail older body could house such awesome power, confidence, and courage? I now believe that the Crone may well represent the successful integration of the Pilgrim, the Seer, and the Sovereign within one person. Soft when she needs to be compassionate, stubborn when she needs to be true to her convictions, and vocal when her heart tells her it is important to speak, the Crone may well be the best example in the world today of where we are headed as a more conscious, more spiritually evolved human species. Many indigenous cultures have recognized this, holding a place of honor for the older women, trusting them to make important decisions such as when and if to go to war and how to settle tribal disputes. I believe that "dangerous older women" are a vast untapped resource of unimaginable magnitude for the world.

The Never Enough culture has deliberately sidelined older women and treated them in a condescending and dismissive way. The emphasis on youth and physical beauty has worn away the self-confidence of many older women and created a generalized sense of dread about growing old. We rarely see older women who actually look like older women on television unless they are part of a pharmaceutical or health insurance ad. But we miss out on a great deal when we make older women invisible or deem them unworthy. So many in the Never Enough culture are hungry for the temperance and groundedness of those who have found a path of grace amid life's trials and tribulations. We miss greeting our own aging with positivity and pride. Imagine how different aging would feel if we held our elders in highest esteem! I once was told that the aging of the body is to allow the primacy of the spirit to take the lead in our lives. The particle yields to the wave; a wave we can leave behind to ripple out widely to others. What a beautiful rewrite of the superficial tapes of the Never Enough culture that are so obsessed with how we look or what we can physically do. The International Council of 13 Indigenous Grandmothers, a group of indigenous elders from all over the world who travel together to share their wisdom, have proven that when older women consciously come together to speak what they know, the world is eager to listen.

Estés's phrase "dangerous old woman" prompted me to ask, Do we have to wait more than fifty years of our life span for the integration of the Crone to appear in us? Is there a shortcut? I suspected that the qualities that make the Crone so valuable are not actually skills we cultivate, learn, or earn over time, but are inherent from birth but become lost through Never Enough cultural conditioning. Crones have somehow learned how to shed layers of conditioning like old coats. My hunch was affirmed when I learned of the work of Jean Liedloff. Essentially, what Jean was able to do was compare the psychology of children and infants of an indigenous tribe that has never abandoned the Enough Story to the children and infants of our own Never Enough culture.

She spent two and a half years in the Venezuelan jungle living with the indigenous Yequana tribes. She found that the parenting practices and attitudes of this peaceful, nonviolent culture were radically different from those accepted as normal in the modern world. In her book *The Continuum Concept*, Liedloff suggests that if our expectations that the world will be responsive and friendly to our needs are not met as infants and toddlers, we tend to compensate for these unmet needs by alternate means throughout life, resulting in many forms of mental and social disorders. In other words, it is more likely that issues such as violence and depression arise because of cultural practices than some kind of inherently troubled or violent aspect of human nature.

While we cannot go back to our infancy and childhood to change how we were raised or rewrite the Never Enough messages we ingested about our worthiness, we can at least now heartily challenge the validity of those messages. One could say that everything we do to "prove" our worthiness throughout life may be our way to compensate for the disconnect between what we inherently knew as children to be true about ourselves as divine, wondrous beings, and what was reflected back to us from a harsh, preoccupied, judgmental, and often stingy Never Enough world. The turnaround comes when we choose to listen to and trust our direct knowing about our wondrous, divine selves and understand that no matter what we do or achieve, the world cannot provide that sense of worth from outside. Our worth can, however, be abundantly sourced from a remembrance that we were born enough and will always be enough.

Expert to Essence

Obviously, societal norms speak loudly, often too loudly, for us to hear our own deeper knowings or to acknowledge them as a primary compass in our lives. There are times, though, when we notice the dissonance between what we deeply know is right and what we observe around us.

A few years ago, I had one of these experiences while attending a conference whose focus was compatible with my futurist, indigenous, and spiritual interests. As I settled into the conference, I noticed something I hadn't expected. Other than during breaks, there was little or no opportunity for participants to actively participate. Basically, it was a conference in which your primary job was to sit quietly in your seat. Whether I was naive or prejudiced by my background in transformational learning, I was deeply disappointed by the design.

One presenter whose work I admired gave a lecture that got me so excited I could hardly contain myself by the end of his talk. His lecture was about the shift of the ages from the perspective of indigenous cultures of the Southwest and Central America. He referred to the dawning age according to the Aztec calendar as "the Age of Great Movement." To close his lecture, he told a story about a set of premature twin babies. One of the twins was near death and the doctors didn't know what to do. A nurse suggested that they break hospital protocol and put the two babies into one incubator together. It worked. With the companionship of his twin, the weaker baby survived. On the large screen in the lecture hall, the lecturer flashed a picture of the two babies in the incubator. He continued the story. One day when the nurse checked on the babies, she found the healthier baby had placed his little arm around the weaker one. Several people in the audience were moved by this photo. You could hear a collective *Aww!* reverberate across the packed lecture hall.

In a lightbulb moment, I made the connection. By "the Age of Great Movement" was he inferring the movement from the head to the heart—as in feeling "moved" by the photo? He hadn't directly said that, so I felt I had uncovered some kind of hidden message he meant to convey. After the lecture, I was able to overcome my shyness and approach him at his book-signing booth. I wanted to ask if he had meant to make the reference to "being moved." He responded in a slightly dismissive, deadpan tone that no, he hadn't thought of it that way. As I wasn't there to get a book signed, his assistant motioned impatiently for the next person in line to come forward. I was devastated. Whether or not he had consciously meant to make the reference, I felt certain that intuitively he included the story about the twins to help his audience make that connection. Rather than welcome the awareness of the synchronicity, he chose to dismiss it.

I later realized that one of the key reasons I attended the conference must have been to experience the inadequacy and disconnection of the expert model. We all suffer when we only accept information and ideas from experts and discount messages that come from those we might refer to as "lesser than." The experience set me on a path of deeper inquiry about what models of gathering would be consistent with the arising culture, which would treat every person as precious and valuable to the whole. In that way, my painful experience at the conference could serve as a catalyst.

What I understand now is that our current system has a very narrow and predictable formula: Experts are placed on a pedestal because it is proven to be profitable. Forced isolation has a purpose: to create and maintain the illusion of superiority and therefore *added value*. If experts were to come off the podium and dialogue as equals with the audience, pretty soon people would not believe that the experts were that special or different from themselves. It was necessary to make the speaker seem like a scarce commodity.

I think we get so used to certain structures such as conferences, and it never occurs to us that we are accepting heart-numbing limitations rather than asking for what we really need and desire. The expert model relies on the false high from a "brush with someone famous." This false high keeps us from noticing that nothing deep or long lasting has occurred as a result of this encounter. Nothing meaningful is drawn out of *us* in this experience, and therefore it is not empowering or lasting.

But what we give up to create that illusion of separation is quite a lot. I can't help but think what a treasure trove an audience is, how a free exchange of ideas, insights, experiences, and reflections could catalyze, enliven, and enrich a speaker's work. How many times do we miss the right piece of information because it doesn't come from where we expect? Egos get hugely activated around the expert model, whether it's the expert's or the audience's. A habit of ranking is the reason. The more the separation, the more the ego becomes activated on all sides. We are all people, and we're all equally deserving of an opportunity to contribute our unique ideas and insights. When we are treated as equals, the ego relaxes, and our authentic essence shines through. We all are the beneficiaries when the collective wisdom is woven and accelerated essence to essence.

The High Price of the Expert Model

We give up more than we realize when we reinforce the expert model. For example, we delay important cures when competing pharmaceutical companies closely guard their research. What if, instead of protecting proprietary information, companies actually worked together with the overall goal of finding a cure as quickly and cheaply as possible? What could happen if a group of scientists agreed to work together across organizational boundaries to solve a problem such as ensuring there is enough clean water for everyone on the planet? This is exactly what happened when a consortium of scientists from universities across Canada combined efforts to invent an inexpensive, lightweight, reusable water purifier utilizing the latest innovations in nanotechnology. It can be done.

What Replaces Pedestals and Hierarchies?

A wisdom circle is the natural form to replace hierarchies and pedestals. Circles support the Enough culture by creating space for the meeting of equals. In circle, people take turns speaking while the rest in the circle deeply listen without comment. As a circle matures, the sharing deepens and trust builds. More essence is shared and affirmed. There is much written about circles, a very ancient practice that is now enjoying a resurgence. (And I go into more depth about circles in chapter 8.) But the important thing is to try one to see for yourself how transformative something as simple as a circle can be.

We are definitely making progress toward inviting essence-to-essence collaboration in our gatherings. For example, the international organization Gather the Women Global Matrix holds all their conferences and events in a circle. Even their teleconferences utilize a "virtual talking stick" to ensure each person is given the space to be heard without interruption. A consortium of women's organizations who meet at the United Nations Commission on the Status of Women each year have loosely formed to advocate for bringing circle practices to the United Nations.

Groups are using a variety of circle methods such as World Café, the Four-Fold Way, Appreciative Inquiry, and the Art of Hosting to facilitate participative group processes. World Café is a structured conversational method designed to encourage open and intimate sharing as small groups and then link ideas within a larger group, harvesting the collective intelligence. The Four-Fold Way is a conversational method developed by Angeles Arrien based on the Native American medicine wheel.

Apprecative Inquiry is an alternative to problem solving that utilizes collective inquiry to form a positive vision of a desired future state that is so compelling it inspires action. Finally, the Art of Hosting uses a blend of these practices along with story-telling to co-create innovation and address complex challenges. What all of these have in common is that they try to move communication and intention to the level of listening for essence. From a place of our common humanity, we create an opportunity for diplomacy and collective action for the greater good.

What we are learning is that the shift of paradigms asks that we align what we do with how we do it. The old Never Enough models of "how" cannot leapfrog us to a new age. They were designed by old assumptions we have outgrown. We must invent and practice new methods, which means leaving our comfort zone and daring to fail. How do we dare to risk looking foolish and failing if we do not invest in containers that allow us to feel safe when we are vulnerable and heard when we are growing into our voice?

As long as there are hierarchies and pedestals, we are not reaching our creative potential as a species. Doors are closed to synergy and cross-pollination of ideas. When we feel we are enough to contribute what we know and understand, a new way of being is called into focus for us—*a great movement from the head to the heart*. When we are self-loving and self-respecting, we reject the habit of giving our power, voice, and authority over to experts. We step into a new pattern of relating as co-creative equals—essence to essence. This is the shift from expert to essence, and it is part and parcel to the emergence of the Enough Story.

Tapping Our Depths

The "I am enough" of the Enough Message is much like a diving board into the deep end of the pool. We only know what is in the depths *after* we've jumped in. If we don't dare to dive deep into our beingness, we will not know what resources are there for us. We will dwell on the surface, where there is great turbulence and seeming chaos and instability. Down deeper in our being we discover peace and wellsprings of joy, creativity, courage, and security we didn't even know we possessed. Without visiting the depths, our tools for transformation are limited. We can try to will ourselves to believe we are enough with mantras and self-help regimens, but we cannot deeply, unshakably *know* that we are enough, that this is the deep down truth of us.

Much has been written about Enough before, but the vast majority of what is written only goes as far as managing our surface behaviors (e.g., how to will yourself to be happier with just enough rather than thinking you need more). It is my hope that we take the "I am enough" instruction as an invitation to stop blaming ourselves for the flaws of culture we have inherited. Without the overlay of shame and guilt, my hope is that we can access more gentleness and self-love for this compelling transition.

Permission Granted

When I made the choice eighteen years ago to be a full-time wife and mother, it was what worked best for my particular family situation; but it wasn't an entirely easy choice. At the time, I was about a month away from securing a promotion to senior management at the organization I had worked in for seven years. I had invested six years earning my bachelor's and master's degrees. When you make the choice that I did to withdraw from the workforce, you risk quite a bit. But you do not stop contributing something valuable. You simply bring your skills to something different. You become attuned to the subtle. You become vigilant for the slight changes in mood, emotion, energy, health, and behavior of those around you. You become deeply aware of the insatiable need for nurturance in our world. Despite this, most of the world takes the work of nurturers for granted, so you have to get used to being invisible as you do these powerful and meaningful things. When you are a full-time nurturer, you know it is deeply challenging and worthwhile work. You know it has the power to transform lives. You realize that the limiting factor in providing nurturance is your ability to draw it up and share it with others. And that is a huge responsibility.

While the feminist movement should have held up the nurturer as someone of deepest value, it ironically chose to do just the opposite, leading to what I see as a mass global divestiture from nurturance in the world. What became important was work, the ability to purchase things, and one's degrees, titles, and power, making it seem perfectly logical to replace what nurturers formerly did with commercialized versions of nurturance, such as day care centers and nursing homes. But the visible, physical things caregivers provide are only a very tiny slice of the pie, the tip of the iceberg of how nurturers actually hold humanity up, how they connect people with the well of spiritual and emotional sustenance they desperately need in order to thrive.

My choice to go against this feminist trend, to do what seemed old-fashioned and backwards, was part personal calling and part conscious protest. I voted with my life for the deeper truth I knew. Nurturers mattered. The extinction of nurturers was harming the status of women. It was diminishing the spirit and resilience of all of humanity. It was accelerating the damage to Mother Earth, the nurturer of all nurturers. Nurturing may not be everyone's role to play in life, but it mattered that someone was doing it and well.

It became my mission to tend a small well of nurturance that people in my life could return to in any moment of need, knowing that they wouldn't ever be turned away. It is in this role that I have received great gratification and meaning. My life has been deep, rich, abundant, and peaceful, my family on solid footing, my relationships connected and alive. But somehow it never seemed to be adequate enough. With so much need in the world, how could I possibly make a dent?

Anytime I had depression or anxiety, the reason was always the same. Echoing in my mind was the thought, "I am overwhelmed. There isn't enough of me to go around." I had, at least for my loved ones, become a rather skilled empath, anticipating and feeling their pain and struggles profoundly, sitting with them to remind them that love and compassion surround them always.

I am also, like many sensitive people, susceptible to absorbing the pain of the world. I tend to experience the waves of despair sweeping the planet whenever there are large natural or economic disasters. As strange as it may seem, I can feel density contained in weather systems—the heavier, more emotionally and chemically laden air from the south sweeping up from the cities along the East Coast, and the significantly lighter and clearer air blowing in from the pristine forests of northern Maine and Canada. Sometimes my physical body will respond to the dense air with sadness, lethargy, headaches, aches, and pains. I would have thought myself crazy were it not for a cluster of "regular" people in my life whose weather-related symptoms almost always mirrored mine. With so much heaviness in the world, it seemed somehow selfish to hold any nurturance back in reserve for myself. It is a classic mistake nurturers make.

When it became too much to keep my heart open to all of this neediness in the world, I would shut down or try to push back the disturbing feelings with all sorts of distractions. My distraction of choice was usually food. I would sometimes inexplicably lose my passion for anything for extended periods of time, going through the motions but losing touch with my own capacity to experience pleasure, hopefulness, or joy. I knew I could not speak of it to my husband or son without them thinking that their love was not enough for me. What I knew was that it had absolutely nothing to do with them or the life we had built together. But trying to convince them of that seemed another unwanted burden for which I had little time or energy.

I knew that my challenge was not taking place where my husband and I have lined up so well, but somewhere else where we didn't share the same language. This was true for many married or partnered spiritual women I knew. Something about what is bubbling up right now in women must be taken care of in a purely feminine place within ourselves, and for this what we need most is the company of other spiritual women. When we cultivate soulful friendships that radiate compassion, non-attachment, and love, we remember how to nurture and love ourselves more faithfully. A circle of spiritual women is a place to directly experience this.

A circle can be as few as two people. My most profound circle has been with my friend Linda. Rarely, if ever, do we give advice to one another. I don't have to work hard to explain myself or worry about startling her with my sorrow or my visions. We are committed to speaking truth and to confronting our own stuck places, asking what we were meant to learn from our deeper questions and struggles. Our code to one another through these spiritual labor pains has been the phrase "I am awake with you." It is a reassurance that has carried me steadily through many spiritual peaks and troughs and given me the boldness to move more swiftly along my inner path of becoming.

My sense is that the pace of becoming is accelerating for most people right now. The key skill in times like these is our ability to let go of limiting patterns, agreements, and beliefs that we co-created long ago but which we no longer need. My agreement as a stay-at-home mom, denying that I had an additional purpose in the world, was one that no longer fit who I was becoming.

I knew what could happen if I ignored my growing edge. I had made the wrong choice in this regard in my early forties, paying a dear price for it: the loss of an ovary and the onset of early menopause. I did not give myself permission to fully expand at that time. I was afraid to. I was truly fortunate to come across *Returning to My Mother's House* by Gail Straub in which she revealed that the same thing had happened to her and to her good friend, Dr. Christiane Northrup. A damaged ovary symbolized blocked creativity and unexpressed feminine energy. For both, the loss of an ovary had become a wakeup call to birth their broader work in the world. Their work turned out to be books, workshops, and lectures that have since benefitted millions of women. I decided to thank my ovary for making the sacrifice that woke me up and vowed to my remaining ovary to change my ways.

As I thought about what to do with my Enough assignment, a story started to unfold in my awareness. I relaxed and let it come through in full color. I saw a forked river whose two tributaries each eventually led to the same lake. A long time ago, one of the tributaries had been dammed up. As a result, the land downstream had become parched and abandoned. The wildlife chose instead to crowd into the smaller area of fertile land around the tributary that was still allowed to flow. Since the land near the flowing tributary was fast being taken over by farmland, the amount of available habitat was always shrinking. Wildlife was disappearing.

Over time, due to the one tributary needing to handle the full force of the water that flowed down from the mountains, its banks had begun to erode. There were frequent floods, washing away crops, roads, and homes. After a particularly bad flood, the villagers gathered to decide what to do. Many of the women and a few men in solidarity with them stepped forward. Their hearts had ached for some time for the land that had been abandoned downstream from the dammed tributary. They had been trying to water it with buckets from the larger river, keeping little patches alive with small gardens of fruits and flowers in hopes of attracting the wildlife back. Might opening the old dam solve two problems at once? The leaders of the village were in fear and scarcity and did not want to hear it. The village had grown, and they believed there wasn't enough water to sustain the land around both tributaries. Surely the farmland that was essential to the well-being of the village wouldn't have enough water if they shared the water with the other tributary. Nothing must be allowed to threaten that.

The leaders of the village put their heads together to focus on ways to control the flow of water and began investigating how to engineer levies and more dams upstream. They discussed stripping the nearby mountain and using the soil to replace the washed out farmland. But the coalition of women and a few men were not convinced and gathered separately in the middle of the night, meeting in circle, asking Spirit to guide their visions and actions. One of the women spoke powerfully about how both tributaries ended in the same lake. Both were part of one story, not two. The needs of one did not diminish the needs of the other. Mother Nature had made both tributaries and her original design could be trusted. Another woman in the group pressed her palms to her chest and spoke with tears in her eyes of how her own body reaffirmed this wisdom. "Would cutting off one leg or one arm make any other part of my body more resilient? My beating heart can feed every part of my body without denying any." Just before dawn, they knew what to do. They went down to the old dam and each removed a single board until the force of the water itself did the rest.

Many years later, the tale was told over and over again how the small coalition of women and men had saved the village, how rotating the crops between old farmland and new had kept the land alive and had doubled the food supply, how wildlife with sufficient territory had multiplied, and how the floods had stopped.

This story was telling me that I had nothing to fear. My family's needs were in fact not in conflict with my call to service in the world. It was only in my mind that the two were separate. No matter if the river or rivers are family obligations, earning a living, or some other commitment you made to someone or something long ago, little buckets are not enough to feed your soul's purpose. But this story is also about the larger story playing out in our world today: the struggle between fear and love; the status quo and nature's wisdom; the head and the heart. I have a knowing that it is perhaps your story, too, an urgent message to water what is parched in *you*.

It is not necessary to starve ourselves of our dreams in the false sense that we are doing anyone any favors. We know it isn't true. We aren't actually playing a zero-sum game at all. We never have been. We are bringing in new potential, new energy, new creativity altogether; and to do this we need to give ourselves permission to remove what blocks us from ourselves. It is not necessary to create small and alone in this way. We weren't meant for alone or small. We are so much more than we've been told. We are enough for everything we've dreamed.

Claim and Liberate

How do we give ourselves permission to unblock what is stuck? In a recent conversation with my friend Linda, I had channeled the word *claim* in response to a challenge she was having. It is a word that has stuck and served us both many times since. I had asked her what it was she was not claiming but wanted to claim in her life. At first she bristled at the word "claim." It sounded foreign—too assertive, too narcissistic, too selfish—and I understood. She was the least selfish person I had ever known. But as we both allowed the word to settle into our awareness, "claim" spoke in a softer, feminine voice with new meaning: letting go of all that prevents us from bringing our fullest power and light to the world. Claiming can mean letting go, a feminine process of surrender, something very different from the masculine interpretation of "claim," which is about taking control. The meaning I was told to convey was specific: claiming one's sovereignty to live one's purpose; no excuses, no holding back, no giving all of ourselves away, but remaining in one's full light and power knowing that this best serves everyone without exception. Claim held a certain "mother bear" fierceness to it, gathering up and protecting that which is fragile and tender, growing and developing until it is strong enough to stand on its own. As is often the case, what I thought was for Linda was also for me. I realized I had not yet fully and powerfully *claimed* my Enough work. I had been timid with it, quietly fitting it between other roles and responsibilities but not claiming it as the soul's calling I deep down knew it to be.

Tears flowed as I allowed myself to deeply face the inner rift I had created between my desires and my fears, realizing how much I desperately wanted to claim my own Enough mission and at the same time how scared I was to do so. Linda mirrored back to me the "mother bear" words that were rising up in defense of my heart-calling. "It is time. Time for the Enough Message. Time for people to claim themselves. Time to give ourselves permission to be in our fullest power and light. It is selfish to let your personal fears hold you back. It is selfish and *wrong*." The enemy, I realized, was my own head, swirling with learned doubts and fears and those supposedly unbreakable and stingy "good girl" rules, agreements, and patterns I had followed my entire life. I needed to trust my heart. I didn't need to starve any part of myself or my dreams. There is enough to nourish all of it.

A new, more finely tuned word bubbled up for me, similar to "claim." My word was "liberate." This word was already personally resonating in my life. It was linked to the heritage and spirit of my country and also to the purest intent of the women's liberation movement. I had even lived for the first eight years of my adult life on a road called Liberty Bell Lane. But liberate was also integral in my roles as a mother and author. "Liberate" means to let out, to release, to set free that which was previously contained. Your creations are not yours to hold back or to hold on to. They have destinies of their own that you cannot control. You must liberate them.

Birth mothers understand the quickening as birth nears, the visceral sense of not being able to hold the new life within one second longer. They also know firsthand the strange in-between of being one with new life, sensing it within you as a potential only you can directly know as real. Birth mothers know the wave of fear that comes when the life they protected within them is suddenly real in the world but so very fragile. I had no choice but to liberate the Enough assignment. Whatever my trepidation, the birth would happen. Enough would become real in the world, and I would stand beside it and nurture it as best I could.

Giving Birth to Ourselves

How many times have we held back offering something because we believed we needed to be perfect first? What we are collectively birthing is not only our authentic work, but also our bigger, more whole selves. Both our selves and our work are co-evolving at the same time. We don't need to be perfect or complete in order to birth new work. In fact, I actually think the journey is more satisfying if we aren't. Claiming our role in birthing something is a calling of the purest kind. It is primal and incorruptible and is in the end about being loyal to that calling above any projections about what others think we should be. It requires deep honesty about our fears and projections, including the fear of failing, or a need to be seen by others as skilled, competent, good, or perfect. All too often, as author Brené Brown reminds us, the fear of looking imperfect and of feeling vulnerable keeps us from daring greatly. But if we are not daring greatly, we may never get to meet our most alive selves or know that we are capable of living a more fulfilling, purposeful life.

We each came here to give birth to something unspeakably precious, something not a single soul could create in the exact way that we can. Our greatest creations are love made manifest. How could something so imbued with love truly be scary, difficult, or wrong? Our fears and self-doubts keep us preoccupied and unavailable to listen for our life purpose. If we sat in stillness more often like the Seer or the Sovereign, we would get the visions we are looking for.

It is your job to claim the space and time to experience yourself as the birth, labor pains and all, and to use what you've experienced to liberate yourself and the world from fear once and for all. What I know is that the birth itself changes you; the beauty and surprise of it, like a baby's crystalline eyes staring back at you, endless pools of love and light that convey everything ever known without a single word. Such things can take your breath away and restore your faith in humanity and yourself in an instant. There is no reason to deny yourself the one profound act of love that would allow you to liberate what you came to liberate from your own loving heart. When your purpose becomes clear to you, and it will eventually, you are enough to live it. You are enough not because you think you have the required résumé, credentials, skills, or experience in hand. Maybe you don't have any of what you thought you needed. Do it anyway. The rules have changed. Enough territory is new territory. In many cases, there is no roadmap yet. You are enough because your purpose calls to you at a deep level you cannot deny. You are enough because if you don't heed the call, you will not have lived fully. It is yours to experience. It is your time. It is why you came. You are enough for this.

I have found that the Enough Message is a love letter and a permission slip to all those who want to participate in remaking our world. The huge task of remaking the world is doable because you are not the only one doing it—and you never have been. Our task is to each remove only a single board, the one that is lodged between our own head and heart. Allow yourself to imagine the rush experienced when the natural flow of the cosmos is restored through your one little action. Hear the *whoosh* as a collective sigh of relief, a collective hallelujah echoed throughout the world as others do the same. Sense the imminent force of nature pushing against what remains of the blocked-up energy. It knows what to do. It has always known what to do, awaiting only our permission to gush forth to take care of the rest.

None of the strategies shared in this chapter would be complete without recognizing that it is through our depths that we are most available to connect with nature's enduring Enough Story and with each other, essence to essence. These strategies move us to a territory outside the constricted box of the old Never Enough Story to recover a deep and personal knowing of our inherent, enduring enoughness.

We are very, very close now.

Will you give yourself this single, profound gift of love?

Will you give yourself permission?

Come,

Awaken from the myth of scarcity.

Claim yourself.

Liberate your gifts.

It has always been your birthright.

You have always been enough for this.

You chose this time.

You chose this place.

You chose to be you.

Remember?

No need to bring fear with you.

I am awake with you.

And you already have everything you need.

It could be the easiest thing in the world.

The thing you most want to do.

It is no longer a secret.

We are here to do the possible, the inevitable.

We are here to remake the world.

6

I Have Enough

I am safe. I have more than I think I have,
enough to thrive, enough to share.

When we lose our sense of belonging, we tend
to fill our lives with belongings.

Our culture lacks a collective understanding of what it means to have not too much, not too little, but enough. We are much more comfortable with the idea of more, more, more and better, better, better. One thing that blocks us from exploring alternatives to Never Enough thinking is the fear that we will be asked to give up what we have. Enough becomes automatically translated somehow into "less than more." But what if enough was truly enough? What if enough was the sweet spot, the "just right" that Goldilocks found so satisfying?

Enough is not a fixed amount, but a highly subjective value. There is no global consensus about what enough is. But what we do know is that in the highly competitive consumerist culture of America, the bar for what constitutes enough is set higher than anywhere else on Earth. We also know that the American measure of enough is severely out of alignment with what is realistic, sustainable, or good for the planet. Rather than go down the road of shame or blame about this, this chapter will explore the root cause of the insatiable hunger for more, the Never Enough worldview itself. We will examine how it keeps us perpetually on the treadmill to obtain enough, prevents us from reaching a state of satiety and satisfaction, and keeps us from noticing the true sources of enoughness within and all around us.

A Tale of More

During the process of writing this book, there was a devastating EF5 tornado in Oklahoma that claimed almost a dozen lives and caused billions of dollars of damage. I, like many people, had a hard time taking my eyes off the unprecedented devastation shown on the television. I watched interview after interview of people whose entire neighborhood had been flattened to the ground, surprised by the resilience and steadiness in their voices and something else I couldn't quite articulate at the time—an uncharacteristic calm?

I remember one particular interview where a reporter was speaking with an older woman who had a peaceful smile on her face. He said something like, "Didn't you tell me this was your dream home and you just moved in six months ago?"

"Oh yes," replied the woman. "I just finished hanging the last curtain."

Obviously perplexed that the woman seemed so serene, he pressed for more emotion. "And you lost your car also? But where will you go now, what will you do?"

The peaceful countenance never leaving her face, she almost looked freed in some way. "My daughter is coming to get me. I've been thinking of moving closer to her anyway."

Why is it that in the face of such overwhelming loss, such devastation, we find that people are capable of accessing a certain kind of peace and grace? Is it that they have discovered, even if for a short time, the secret that they are not their stuff, that life is what is precious, that they can let go of what they owned and still be all right? Are they able to glimpse the gift of knowing they are still here, and because they are still here, they are perfectly enough?

It seems we will be experiencing an increase in devastating storms due to global warming, and so these lessons about our attachment to our possessions are touching more and more of us, not just directly but through the stories and images shared through the media. Could it be we all are being nudged to examine our relationships with our possessions and to see what again and again pulls people up from this kind of devastation isn't clinging to our possessions but loving well and belonging to a caring community?

I can't help but think it wasn't a coincidence: the name of the town devastated by the tornado was Moore, Oklahoma.

Enough Is Not Austerity

In these times of global economic constriction, it is easy to label any kind of cutting back as something to be feared or resisted. Our idea of letting go of old standards of enoughness is inevitably tied to images of loss, shame, grieving, collapse, and failure. This is letting go by constriction, by submitting to becoming "smaller." It is associated with disempowerment and a loss of control over our outer circumstances. This kind of letting go is a major recurring headline in our world today in the form of "austerity measures," "failing economies," "housing bubbles," and "stock market crashes." This is when letting go is imposed upon us, when what we may lose are our nest eggs, homes, or critical services such as health care, food, transportation, or housing assistance. To be clear, being forced to cut back on basic needs is not at all what I mean by Enough.

Inner Enoughness = Real Abundance

We see how the Never Enough culture adds to our insecurity and fear by placing such a strong emphasis on what we own. William Wordsworth seemed to be pointing to this when he said, "The world is too much with us . . . Getting and spending, we lay waste our powers." When we think that our value and our power are derived from the things we possess, we fear that these things could be taken away from us at any time through a job loss, a divorce, a natural disaster, a poor financial decision, or an expensive health crisis. This is a very insecure way in which to live, and it robs us of energy, autonomy, and happiness. The acquisition of more and more things and our growing insecurity about protecting what we have become a vicious cycle that prevents us from making a commitment to align with the richness and solidity of our inner lives. The goal, then, is to feel the life that we are as fully as possible, to source our happiness, security, and sense of meaning first and foremost from within. This is freedom from the hamster wheel. This is taking back our power. This is Enough.

By Enough I am not advocating some kind of forced austerity or simplification of lifestyle to appear socially responsible or virtuous. True, when we shift to an inner feeling of Enough, we find that we naturally crave less stuff around us. Our craving subsides because we have broken through the illusion that possessions and achievements are what make us feel enough. The Enough Message and abundance are not mutually exclusive. The Enough Message is about feeling our inner sufficiency, which leads to being receptive to magnetizing all kinds of appropriate and useful abundance to our lives. It is about having enough of the things that are meaningful and enlivening for us and not too much of the things that weigh us down and keep us too busy or stressed to enjoy our lives.

For life to have meaning, for it to have a charge to it, we are motivated to create, experience, or obtain things that we do not currently have. Humans are creator beings. We are drawn to novelty, and if we are deprived of it we can become depressed or physically ill. This creative spirit is not only universal and inherent; it is the source of much pleasure and satisfaction. We could go as far as to say that attraction is the "stuff" of the universe, the evolutionary force that moves through in the form of our own passion and creativity. Our enough naturally includes what we are passionate about—our hobbies, something of beauty, something that helps us to grow or to better express ourselves. All of these forms of enough serve us and the world.

But there is a different kind of enough that is manufactured by the Never Enough worldview. It is a kind of generic, prescribed, or coerced list of things that supposedly leads to us experiencing love, acceptance, and social status. This kind of social pressure to obtain more things isn't good for us or for the planet. It places a heavy burden on natural resources and does not lead to lasting contentment. It is important for us to be able to distinguish this list of generic things from what arises from our authentic selves as a core passion or need.

Avoiding the "I Never Have Enough" Trap

What we truly long for is a lasting experience of inner contentment and sufficiency. Although we may realize from experience that possessions rarely live up to this standard, we are still buying into the Never Enough illusions and traps. Why? We tend to blame ourselves for our unhappiness, thinking we must work harder or search farther for the next shiny object that will finally succeed in satisfying our hunger. The ego is far less precise than the heart. It will settle for having anything that is immediate, easy, safe, and impulsive or generally considered "better" rather than to bring us what it is we really need. The heart, if we tuned in, would identify precisely what it is that makes us flutter and come alive. It would guide us to experience what it is we do need. The ego gets hooked by the temptation or flavor of the day, making us believe the generic path is our path to happiness and success. Cultural scripts, sales pitches, fads, and norms create an overwhelming flood of messages to convince us to keep searching and striving among the generic must-haves and must-dos that are not based in any kind of real need or utility.

When we feel we need external markers to be worthy of love and acceptance, we are covering up a wound rather than healing it. We may have been taught that we must earn acceptance and love through outer achievement and things, but when we buy into this idea we will never know the answer to our central questions, "Am I loved for my achievements and things, or for simply being me? Am I enough?" Nothing outside of us can replace self-acceptance and self-love. This is why, I believe, the Enough Message begins with "I am enough." It is our first step in the process of transforming our lives and the world. When we get in touch with how precious and irreplaceable we are, we are more likely to give ourselves permission to depart from the generic "must-haves," enabling us to focus on what truly brings us a lasting sense of meaning and happiness. And this leads to us being of greatest service to the world.

A second issue is that Never Enough thinking always sets up a competitive dynamic. We may receive a bump in self-esteem when we advance in the social strata, but when we improve our own situation without improving the situation of others, we can never live in a world that is truly peaceful, internally or externally. What we get in equal measure is a bump in self-esteem and a combination of guilt that we may not deserve what we have or insecurity that we may lose what we have. We haven't advanced at all. We will repeatedly be faced with questions such as when to share with others and if so, how much. We are forced in this scenario to self-protect or to see ourselves as somehow different or superior to those who have less. If we lose what we have, we feel diminished and ashamed.

A friend of mine recently spent a month volunteering in South Africa. When she returned, I asked her what surprised her the most on the trip. "The heavily fortified homes of the rich," she said, describing all manner of barbed wire, security cameras, and concrete enclosures on residential properties. "I couldn't help but wonder who was more free, the poverty-stricken outside the walls of the mansions or the people living in the mansions."

When our orientation arises not from our possessions or sense of entitlement, but instead from a sense of inner enoughness, there is no possible downside. When what we need is contained within us, any possible failure or delay in exterior circumstances cannot diminish who we are. We are more willing to take risks, to share, and to live with much less. All experiences both pleasant and unpleasant are part of our journey, all are necessary to where we are going. We are in this case always advancing, if not accelerating.

When we realize that we are enough, what motivates us is no longer to fill an inner void but to express ourselves through our passions and gifts in a way that is aligned with the world's needs. We don't need to take ourselves so seriously and we don't need to sit in the driver's seat or take credit, for the joy is in the doing. We are in a mode of connection, freedom, flow, and service. Because the universe is wondrous and its potential to work with us vast, we will repeatedly be delighted and surprised by what presents itself as matches for our passions. This truly is a rich and abundant life!

Considering that we may be inherently Enough can be an eye-opening revelation at first. It may be difficult to imagine a world without the old self-judging inner chatter and without a need to prove that we are better than everyone else. Without these scripts, it becomes peaceful and quiet inside. We experience inner freedom. Our ability to concentrate and focus grows. Without the inner judge peering over our shoulders to question our choices and to critique our performance, we can enjoy what we are doing. We can be fully engaged in the now.

To Have Enough, Let Go

These scripts have also held us back in another way, actually preventing us from living our highest and best lives. When we hold on too tightly to outcomes and goals, we miss many of the ways the right opportunities could possibly come to us. We overmanage, overcontrol, overworry. We force things to come together before their time. As a result, what we allow is usually not as good as what *could* be. All of our cultural and personal conditioning act to pigeonhole our expectations and therefore flatten our trajectory. To free ourselves from settling for the mediocre, the Never Enough we are taught to expect because we are not enough to deserve better, we must let go of limiting messages and take what is commonly known as a leap of faith into the trajectory we want.

We often hear stories of how it takes a major life event to wrest ourselves from our set patterns and ruts, a stroke of luck, a startling health diagnosis, a chance meeting, an epiphany, an accident, or the loss of a job. Whether we initially saw the event as good or bad, the result was setting us on a new and unexpected path that even we could not have predicted. In *The Power of Now*, Eckhart Tolle tells a story of how his journey as a global spiritual teacher did not begin until he gave up trying to resist or manage his severe depression. In so many ways, we allow our habits and the patterns of expectation they create to set a very narrow agenda for our lives. If we want a life that looks discernibly different, we must be willing to look at the deeper patternmakers and realize they are not who we are.

How We Block Receiving What We Really Want

Chances are, if I asked you what you don't have enough of, you would probably be able to produce a list of several things easily. And for each item you don't have enough of, you would probably be able to produce a list of reasons for why you don't have them. Years ago, I was taught a helpful exercise developed by Peter Senge, author of *The Fifth Discipline*, called the Five Whys. The purpose of the exercise is to reveal to yourself the core beliefs you are holding—not to judge them, but to make them visible to you. Here is an example of what doing so might look like: Let's say a woman, Allison, has decided she'd like to make a career change. She's currently a secretary at an insurance company, but she'd like to go back to school to become a teacher. The only problem is that her salary isn't enough to cover her current expenses plus tuition.

> *Not Enough statement: I don't have enough money to go back to school to become a teacher.*
>
> *Why? Because my house and car payments are too high.*
>
> *Why? Because I bought a house and a car that were outside my budget.*
>
> *Why? Because I thought it would make me happy and fulfilled to do so.*
>
> *Why? Because I thought having these things was the source of my happiness.*

Why? Because I wasn't happy with me.

Why? Because what I really want, what I really need to be happy with me, is to follow my calling to become a teacher.

What have I learned from this exercise? That what I know would truly make me happy is to follow my dream of becoming a teacher. Since my house and car have not brought me the sense of fulfillment I thought they would, I can choose to let go of them or downsize in order to do whatever I have to do to pursue my dream.

I invite you now to fill in this sentence: "I don't have enough _____." Try running it though the Five Whys. What did you discover about the underlying reasons why you might not seem to have enough?

An exercise like this can help us not only identify the hidden abundance in our lives, the leverage for getting what we *really* want, but also discern the type of abundance that would bring us the most satisfaction. It is sometimes not that we *can't* afford to have what we want, but that our resources are tied up somewhere else or in something we either no longer need or value. The Five Whys may alternately help us to discover that we have not yet fully committed to ourselves and to our passion. We either have not felt worthy (not Enough) or we are holding on to other life commitments instead.

My Enough Is Not the Same as Your Enough

As the Five Whys exercise demonstrates, it takes a significant amount of courage not only to examine our thinking but also to claim it in the real world as our truth. When we examine our thinking through the Five Whys, we often find that considering "the unthinkable" is the doorway to our freedom. In our example, the unthinkable was to consider downsizing in order to afford tuition. By feeling the truth of how much becoming a teacher means, Allison came to the realization that it is worth the temporary blow to her self-image and lifestyle to make whatever changes necessary to pursue her true calling. She feels into a sense of rightness in the decision, a sense of empowerment and freedom, and ego-based concerns about what others will say fade into the background. The turnaround is when she discovers that *she can—at any time—trade something she already has for something she wants want even more.* This can mean a material object or her time, as in getting a temporary or part-time second job or applying for a grant to fund her dream.

Only when we believe we are enough will we allow ourselves to have enough. By enough, I don't mean the generic version of enough that is defined by someone else. When you realize the world has an investment in each one of us being all we can be and having what we need to fulfill our unique mission, you will no longer think it is selfish to put your enough first. You'll be able to relax into the truth that your enough can and should be different from anyone else's enough. The expectations of others come to mean less and less. Ironically, when you follow your own definition of enough, you boost the chance that you will end up giving maximum value to the world.

Staying in the Flow of Abundance

As an advocate for women's leadership, I have been involved in many nonprofit women's organizations over the years. The difficulty of securing adequate funding almost always comes up. While there are many reasons why women's philanthropy lags behind men's, such as income inequality between women and men, there seems to be another dimension that is psychological. Women oftentimes feel apologetic to their families if they want something that does not directly benefit or relate to family members, and they may find it difficult to ask for what they want. Many women feel they exist on the fringe of their family budgets, and not in the flow of it. This is a matter of gender roles and self-esteem. As a stay-at-home mom for sixteen years, I certainly have experienced this one personally.

My husband has never said no to what I'd like to spend as a volunteer or to a donation I'd like to make, but I tend to feel tight about it anyway. What is this internal tightness, and where does it come from?

As a woman, I have been socialized to devote most of my life to giving to family and friends. I find that I have been much more comfortable as a result with giving rather than receiving. So giving is clearly not the problem. The problem, I believe, is that my interest in women's leadership comes from a place in me that is independent of my family's direct interests. To ask my family to support the organizations I care about is to ask them in a sense to support *me*. The tightness I have felt comes from a place in me that does not feel worthy of receiving. This is choosing to separate myself from the flow, where I neither have the opportunity to receive nor to contribute what I really could. It has been a slow learning process to feel more comfortable asking for my needs and desires to be met. Unapologetically claiming the time and resources I need to participate in my volunteer activities and to write this book has been one of my biggest Enough initiations.

Any number of fears or blocks can keep us from giving what we could be giving to the efforts we care most about. Are we responding to cultural conditioning that makes us feel too insecure financially to give? Do we have a target number in our minds about how much we should have in savings before we feel free to give? Or is it deeper than that? Have we ingested separatist judgments from the Never Enough Story that say each person must fend for themselves no matter what, so we are under no obligation to help? Have we stepped out of the flow of giving and receiving, accepting a colder and more insecure reality than we want?

Living in Maine, I have found drivers on the Maine roads and highways to be patient and polite for the most part. Merging is mostly stress-free. People pause and wave you into the lane. Such everyday kindness gives you a feeling that all is right with the world. I recently was driving with my family to an event in the heart of Boston. I witnessed a number of unkind acts that added significantly to the blockage of traffic. Many drivers were noticeably stressed and were leaning on their horns. By the time we got to the event, my nerves were frayed. Since I refuse to believe that people who live just a little over an hour away from me could be that different, what was going on?

What I understand now is that the flow we experience as a society is up to us. Kindness places us in the flow. What takes us out of the flow? Fear. Judgment. Impatience. Our stories that the world is out to get us. These are all ideas generated by the Never Enough worldview. The greater the traffic or the more stressful the situation, the more we are convinced that the Never Enough Story is right, confirming our certainty that our needs will not be met. We switch into self-protective scarcity mentality. We get aggressive, take what we want without regarding others. We compete. But what happens is that we interfere with the natural flow when we do this. We are contributing to a culture in which our needs will not be met because we are acting in a way that chooses and perpetuates separation.

As I have done more Enough work, I have learned to confront my own ideas of separation, unworthiness, and lack one by one. I realize it is not necessary to hold my family separate from my charitable or career goals. They are not in reality mutually exclusive. I add value to my family through my work. I now regularly help my husband and son to know that they are supporting a better world by supporting my work. My gratitude gives them a chance to feel connected to the meaning and value their support generates not just for me but also for a wider world. I give them a chance to feel the flow of loving intent that moves through us as a family unit.

No More Deficit Spending

When we're out of the flow, we fear we won't get what we really want and need, so we act in ways that prevent the community and planet from getting what it needs. Conversely, when we act as martyrs or heroes, we tend to give from a place of obligation or ego, creating a feeling of depletion inside. When what we give out is not fully returned, energy feels as though it has been extracted from us. We become drained and sometimes resentful. This feels awful. The issue in both these situations is that we are holding ourselves as separate from the Enough flow around us. When we first place ourselves in the flow, feeling our deservedness, what we attract is affirmation that we are enough and we have enough. When we come from a place of inner abundance, the flow to others becomes natural. We are willing to say no when we need to. When we do feel called to give, we are able to do so wholeheartedly without creating an inner deficit.

Can we see how giving from depletion is a zero-sum game? We aren't really moving anything forward. We are just leaking energy, depleting our health and vitality. It looks and feels a lot like deficit spending. When we take responsibility for speaking up for our needs, we are filling ourselves up first. We become generators of abundance that can be shared without causing sacrifice. We are teaching others how to break free from "deficit spending." Giving feels good again and feeds our energy. We are creating a net positive, new value and energy for the world that has never been here before.

⏤ 7 ⏤

We Are Enough

*I don't need to do it alone anymore. Together we
are capable and strong.*

*I pin my hopes to quiet processes and small circles, in which
vital and transforming events take place.*
—Rufus Jones

In this chapter, I will share a few stories about social movements that are shaping the future through the principle of Enough for everyone. Though these stories represent the growing edge of human social invention at this time, there are many dynamics still in place in the Never Enough culture at large that tend to prevent us from moving gracefully from me to we. The five-sentence Enough Message contains a rhythm, a cadence of inner focus, outer focus, inner focus, outer focus. (I am, I have, we are, we have.) I believe this was to offer us an intentional process for loosening our bonds to these old, constricted dynamics, a path to grace. This chapter will focus on the inner territory that allows us to move more comfortably and confidently into becoming a "we" as groups, neighborhoods, organizations, and communities. We will explore doorways to accessing the kinds of connection, community, love, and support we truly long for.

Remnants of Repeat

Whether we realize it or not, many very old remnants of the Repeat culture are still heavily influencing our social systems and psyches. They must be purged in order to more fully integrate Share principles into our culture. These ideas of separation and judgment cloud our ability to see the potential for synergy and unity that are all around us and within us. And because it is through unity that we receive the security and belongingness we long for, it is worthwhile to challenge anything that keeps us from it. Below is a list of some of these old ideas of separation and unworthiness:

- A habit of ranking ourselves as "lesser than" or "better than" other people

- A culturally reinforced idea of "survival of the fittest" that drives competition

- Past experiences that have taught us we cannot trust other people to have our best interests at heart

- Mass desensitization to violence and emotional drama

- The social sanctioning of martyrdom and selflessness

- The ego overstepping its role—from keeping us safe to reinforcing sameness

- Shaming and blaming instead of claiming what we want

The Gift of Paradox

When we experience a shift in consciousness, paradox is usually at the center. We often find that the exact opposite of what we have been taught is closer to the truth. In an aha moment, it becomes suddenly clear to us. In the case of the shift from me to we, we've been taught to self-protect in ways that keep us isolated and vulnerable, and we've been taught to share in ways that diminish our power and autonomy. For example, survival of the fittest teaches us to compete even when it would be better for us and for everyone involved to collaborate. Martyrdom asks us to share, but in ways that causes us personal suffering and depletion. How do we navigate our way through such complex territory without becoming depleted or isolated?

Discernment and Judgment

I believe the key to unlocking this mystery is to make a clear distinction between discernment and judgment. When we judge, we are in our heads, creating boxes that sort out much of what is going on around us, often unconsciously. When we judge, our decisions can't help but be corrupted by our previous experiences, prejudices, and choices. If we have weeded out a piece of data before, we will do it again. While this may serve to keep us safe, it also keeps us rather stuck in place, repeating the same patterns and perceptual errors again and again. Staying stuck may be fine if we like where we are, but when where we are is not where we want to be, we must call upon new skills and strategies to help us to boldly move forward to where we want to go. When the boat is sinking, as is the Never Enough culture, staying stuck means we go down with the ship.

When we discern instead of judge, we are in our hearts instead of in our heads, open to everything, but keenly sensing what in our experiences are most alive for us. The difference here is that with judgment, we are looking for sameness and predictability to make us feel safe—protection. Through discernment, we are looking for the feeling of a spark, or what unifies us with what shows up in our environment—connection. Sometimes the spark is newness and excitement, and sometimes it is a felt sense of unity and familiarity, something I refer to as resonance or coherence. Through discernment, we are leaving the door open to curiosity, novelty, and risk-taking until we have chosen what feels right for us. Judging would not allow this period of indecision and exploration. It would close the door as soon as possible. Therefore, judging limits our options. Discernment means we trust our hearts to identify the right things for us amid many options and possibilities. We leave the door ajar.

Judging is also tied to our tendency to be tightly wedded to our stories. Lonely stories such as *They're out to get me. I'm not good enough. Nobody likes me. I'm not qualified. I can only rely on myself. Nobody cares about my needs. I'm ugly. They probably think I'm stupid. They're better than me. I'm better than all of them. I'm nobody until somebody loves me. I'm a failure. I'll show them who's boss. I'm all alone in this world.*

These are all stories of separation that cause tremendous suffering. They make us draw back into a stance of self-protectionism. We feel betrayed, misunderstood, disregarded, under attack, and small. Our belief in any of these stories is based on the idea that we cannot ultimately trust the world to support and love us. (There is Not Enough support and love for me.) This is a natural response to a Never Enough culture that perpetuates this story, generating plenty of concrete evidence we can hang on to. But in hanging on to the fallout of the Never Enough Story, we miss quite a bit of what else is there. We forget that these are all just stories. We emotionally respond to them as if they are ultimate truths. Couldn't it be just as likely they aren't true? What data are we systematically weeding out and ignoring that could tell a completely different story, an Enough Story?

Rather than go through the lengthy process of debunking all our stories of separation one by one, I believe there is a shortcut. Enough asks us to move our attention from our heads to our hearts. It asks us to orient toward what we *do* want rather than what we don't. It asks us to look for connections rather than what separates us. What we pay attention to grows. As we look for connections and indulge our curiosity about the richness and potential in those connections, we participate in crafting the web of support we have always longed for.

As discussed earlier, Enough asks us to be the first recipients of our own love, not the last. No more "deficit spending." This means we have to overcome the norm that says it is somehow selfish or desperate to ask for or claim what we need and want. When we understand that love is not a transaction, we no longer need to wait in a codependent way for others to notice us or to bring us love. When we are waiting, we feel small and vulnerable. We may indulge our resentment, self-loathing, and hopelessness. We don't need to play games or create drama in order to generate proof that we are loveable. When was the last time you asked for a hug instead of waiting patiently for someone to notice you needed one? When was the last time you respected your inner boundaries by saying no when you really wanted and needed to? When we believe love and respect only come to us through others, we may not realize it, but we are actually treating people as objects, a means to an end. Even if we aren't consciously aware of what we are doing to manipulate the situation, I do believe our subconscious is aware, and it registers as transactional love and transactional respect rather than the real thing. We are choosing to cut ourselves off from real love. No wonder we feel so lonely!

I am by no means saying it is simple to rewrite these tapes and break these dependencies. Many people carry very deep, old wounds we must never minimize or deny. I am not advocating sweeping them under the rug in any way. But I believe it is through taking the risk of being vulnerable and asking directly for what we need in the here and now that we break through to more intimacy and true unity. We dispel the stories by creating a now that feels better. At the core of our essential selves we all long for the same things: peace, security, love, acceptance, meaning, and respect. The underlying unity is already there. As we gather to tell our stories of vulnerability and to ask for what we need and want, we connect essence to essence, meeting in the unity. We find the vein of truth that we all share. Ego-based boundaries and separation fall away when we are connected essence to essence. We encourage one another to consciously cultivate the richness we seek: inner peace, inner security, self-love, self-acceptance, self-respect, deep meaning, and purpose.

Readying Ourselves for the "We"

The function of the ego is to place order on the vast world before us so we can reduce our stress, avoid danger, and clarify our options—in other words, feel safe. Ego for these purposes is essential and serves the greater good. The problem comes when we allow ego to overstep its basic function by imposing order that is neither necessary nor accurate. In the ego–mind's eye, we perceive that there are those who are both "higher" than us and those who are "lower." We seek our comfort zone based on this perceptual ranking, seeking to reduce risk by finding those who seem by all external indicators to be "most like us." When we do this, we severely limit the possibilities that can unfold in our lives, and the benefits of diversity are lost. We create structures, barriers, and divisions that don't need to be there. It is ego whether we are acting upon assumptions that we are "lesser than" or "greater than" someone else. How do we spring ourselves from such a trap?

Quantum physicist David Bohm points toward a possible answer. Bohm studied what he calls the implicate order, or "the unbroken wholeness of the totality of existence as an undivided flowing movement without borders." You might think of it as a symphony of sound, or a spectrum of color. Underlying everything, the world is connected. Supposed boundaries fade into one another.

Navigating by Resonance

If the ego-mind imposes a false sense of separation that isn't actually there, how do we better sense the order that is there—the implicate order? One way is to listen for the resonance between us in the form of what arises in our environment, whether it's people or ideas. What do I mean by listening for resonance? Let's say you are developing a new charitable venture. As you do so, certain people and ideas enter your world. Perhaps you turn on the TV and a celebrity says something that aligns with your plan. A friend calls, and she has run into an old friend of hers who now runs a foundation that is interested in causes like yours. On social media, someone shares a quote and it reminds you to revisit a book you read ten years ago. All of these things can be seen as synchronicities, and they are much more than that. When we perceive our world as helpful and connected, we begin to see how we are constantly both broadcasting and receiving energy waves with a specific vibratory signature. When resonance between our vibration and the vibration of someone or something in our environment match, we notice and have an opportunity to connect. So often our ego intervenes to shut off this connection. In the example of the celebrity on TV, the ego may prohibit you from feeling you are "big" enough to contact them. If we allow ourselves to listen for the resonance, which we do with our hearts, our intuition, our third eye, we would realize that there is no actual inequality between us and the celebrity, but instead an implicate order of resonance. There is an alignment that is being invited, so if egos can be put aside, a mutually enriching partnership is possible. This is the implicate order, because it is sensing where your unique "color" or "tone" resonates or blends with another in perfect harmony.

Common Ground Is Sourced from Essence

The beauty of relating from our depths (heart) rather than from our outer image or labels (ego/mind) is that we are much more likely to stumble upon common ground. During a political election, for example, a huge magnifying glass is placed on perceived differences, and common ground is completely ignored. Candidates are encouraged to make the ideas of their opponents seem dangerous and radical. It is almost impossible to not become a witness to an angry debate during campaign season, and if we do become personally involved, we could risk damage to long-term relationships with friends, coworkers, and relatives. Can we appreciate the paradox that the very system we rely upon to find common ground is built upon the exact opposite—a model of extreme separation? It is quite clear that we cannot get there from here. Government can only be effective if we lead with our essence. Our essence is that part of us that orients toward our common interests, feels the resonance, and responds with understanding and compassion for the greater good.

When I realize I am enough, and you realize you are enough, there no longer is an urgency in me to convince you to believe what I believe. I don't need you to validate me. I don't need you to agree with me for my world to be okay. I don't need to upstage or demean anyone else. I am whole and full no matter what you think of me or my ideas. We can relax into what connects us, and let the rest be what it is.

Trusting the Process

As human beings in a Never Enough fear-based culture, we tend to be heavy-handed in our attempts to exert control over what is unfolding. We do this whether what we are attempting to control is our lives, the people we know, or the world at large. We have a learned tendency to project our preconceived ideas and expectations onto outcomes, shutting down many more ideal possibilities before they fully have a chance to arise. The need to control is rooted in an underlying lack of trust. We do not believe the universe is fundamentally supportive of our needs. We think we live in a hostile environment that must be manipulated and controlled in order to meet our needs. When we control, we are motivated by fear, so we push away not only what we don't want but at the very same time what we *do* want. What is created is usually some "safe" version of something we have done before. Out-of-the-box thinking is not supported, and we get mired in the need for approval, the need for everyone to be in agreement. If we instead believed in natural self-organization, perhaps we would see that the universe is not hostile but is always ready to partner with us if we let it. We can relax into what is naturally arising because we are trusting that what is right will invariably emerge if we allow it to. It also means we don't need to force or push, but simply yield to divine timing and to a felt sense of when the energy is there to support our next steps. This is a very different way of creating than we are used to, a more feminine approach, but it is a way to minimize suffering and unnecessary mistakes and ensure the kinds of outcomes that are aligned with the greater good of all.

My most powerful and painful Enough initiation was about this very thing. My volunteer work led me to a woman from another part of the country who shared many of my same interests. After we met in person at an event, it was not long before we decided to work together on a project, each bringing something very different but complementary to it. One of my jobs was to try to blend both of our offerings together into a coherent whole, which was at times quite challenging, especially from a distance. My solution was to be clear in demarcating which parts of the project were hers and which were mine, a decision she also supported, as it gave us each some autonomy. Although the project started as a volunteer project, over time we had begun envisioning something that could develop into a possible business. After two years of working part time from our homes to develop the idea, we submitted a draft of the project to a company we hoped would back us.

The company rejected our overall proposal but was interested in the part of the project that I had developed. My partner and I handled this news very differently. I felt it was a huge step in the direction of our dreams to have captured the interest of one of the top companies in its field, a field in which we had no prior experience ourselves. I offered a proposal to her in which I would develop the idea with the company as they requested, then use that foothold and relationship to move her part of the project forward as well. We could continue to work together on workshops and retreats, doing that without a need for backing because I would reinvest the revenues from my project in whatever we would create together.

I didn't expect what happened next. She could not go into trust with me or with the company. She saw my proposal to her as a betrayal, not as an offer of solidarity. When we realized that our approach to business and partnerships was worlds apart, our relationship quickly deteriorated. After I came out of the shock of what had happened, I realized that no one can make anyone do anything, least of all trust another person. The only thing I could control was what I myself would learn from this painful experience.

I went into deep reflection and realized what I had been given was a chance to confront a lifelong pattern that had been keeping me from expressing myself fully in the world. As a relationship person, I had always sought out work partners rather than develop projects completely on my own. As I looked at the pattern, I saw that I usually sought out partners out of fear and insecurity. I would look for an extrovert, a buffer zone, someone more assertive than me to keep me and my idea safe. But by always deferring to someone else in this way, I was avoiding growing those same qualities in myself. I was avoiding doing the inner work I needed to do to claim my wholeness.

During the month the partnership was teetering, I quite literally felt sick to my stomach most of the time. A dark and disturbing cloud seemed to have descended over me, something I recognize now as my own inner resistance to changing a life pattern that had been with me for so long. I did not want to have to do the difficult thing, the thing my inner self knew I needed to do, because it went against all my "good girl" people pleasing conditioning. I didn't want to hurt or disappoint anyone. I didn't want to be labeled heartless and selfish. And I was afraid of standing completely alone. I've never felt so vulnerable and scared. But I knew going out on my own was the only thing I could do to be in truth with myself, the only way I could restore my sense of inner peace. It was an initiation I needed to go through.

Taking responsibility for my life lesson, I walked away quietly and surprisingly without the need to engage in drama or blame. What I felt was gratitude for my partner for offering me this lesson. Had she accepted my proposal, I might have missed my lesson. But because she rejected my offer, I realized that I was willing to give up the project altogether to be in harmony with myself. I did give it up, but then six months later something unexpected happened. The very friends I thought for certain I would lose by making this choice showed up for me and encouraged me to keep going as a solo project. I eventually did so and gained the company's support as well.

In times of inner or outer change, it is easy to let our decisions be determined primarily by our worst fears and self-doubts or by our conditioning of what we must do in order to be regarded well. We get swept up into the stories of why we cannot change our stuck patterns, stories that put everyone and everything, even our egos, above our own inner peace and inner truth. We pay a huge price whenever we try to cope with something we know does not sit peacefully within us. All the energy we expend trying to make the pieces fit together would be better spent investing in standing in our calm center and listening more deeply to who we are and what we truly want—and then trusting what we hear.

A metaphor has been very helpful to me in envisioning this process. I imagine how it feels to sit in the calm center of a hurricane, the world of complication, fears, doubts, manipulations, panic, and drama swirling all around me, but not touching me. While in the center, I feel grounded, safe, clearheaded, and calm. All of that debris is at arm's length. In my mind's eye I observe it swirling by but realize I do not need to judge it or get swept up in it. If I do find myself being drawn into it, I remind myself that the calm center is always waiting for me and I can return to it as often as I like. I can exit the turbulence, and when I do I can see more clearly what is true for me and what is not. I can glimpse the throughway to my most authentic self.

I believe we are supposed to consciously choose the calm center, because when we do, we create alignment between the outer world and our inner needs and values. If you think about it, the outer swirl of a hurricane acts as a giant centrifuge. In science, a centrifuge is used to separate elements of different densities from a liquid compound. Think about it. Separation. In the calm center is the opposite of separation: perfect stillness, a place immune from the forces that would work to pull apart and separate. In the center is communion. We touch what is most universal, real and based in love, including self-love. And because this is so, what we create there naturally creates a world that works for everyone.

We have been taught by the Never Enough paradigm to see the world through a lens of winners and losers. We may assume that standing up for our needs means someone else must pay the price for our happiness. Many of our codependent patterns arise from this unfounded fear. I believe there is always an alignment and right timing in all our partnered life lessons. We are here to liberate one another as we liberate ourselves. When we "get" the lesson that is in a situation for us, we actually are increasing the chances that the other person will "get" the lessons they came here to learn for themselves. Even if this effect doesn't become clear for that person for years (or ever), I believe that claiming inner peace and self-love always contributes to helping others to claim inner peace and self-love as well.

Is It Really Yours to Do?

To be able to feel safe and relax into the calm center, it is important to cultivate a sense of our place in the whole. As mentioned earlier, becoming more aware of our divine gifts and our passions greatly assists us in feeling we are enough. The world is very complex, so it is easy to be drawn away from our center by all the choices offered to us. If an idea comes to us or to someone who's part of a group we are in, we may think this means we have to be the one who implements it. Sometimes it is, but sometimes it isn't. I have learned it is better to pause and deeply reflect, "Is this *your* work to do?"

Unfortunately, the ideas that tend to pop into my head are rarely small. Each would require a full-time commitment. My response to this in the past was to feel like a coward and a failure. The ideas felt like burdens, a mounting to-do list piling up. So I'd store them up for some future time when I felt "big" enough or energized enough to carry them out. That time usually never came. I'd be frustrated, disappointed in myself, and jealous whenever I'd later see someone else actually carrying out "my" ideas in the real world. A needy place inside me, full of shame, would cry out, "But I had that idea first!"

I now realize that most "downloads" are more similar to a robocall than a person-to-person phone call. Many people are receiving the same signals from our world and coming to the same conclusion at approximately the same time. We are waking up to certain potentialities together. We are sensing into the implicate order of the universe, the collective unconscious, the morphogenetic field, because a critical number of us have developed a keener sense of what naturally comes next.

The Enough Message was the one download from all that I had received in my lifetime that captured me completely. I thought, "Oh, now I get it! *This* is how it's supposed to feel when it is *my* work to do!" While I was not happy at all that it took forty-eight years to get my first real assignment, at least I knew I could at last throw out my piles of to-do lists with no guilt at all. What I have learned and what I would like to share is that it is worth it to wait for the one idea that you cannot deny. When our lives are too busy with trying to do too much, we aren't available when the right idea comes along.

When an idea pops into the morphogenetic field for all to access, I think of this as mirroring nature's tendency to produce more than enough, such as when an oak tree drops thousands of acorns each year. Only a few acorns actually take root as a tree. Others become nourishment for squirrels and chipmunks. Others simply feed the ground. I realize that our true inner work when receiving messages from the field is to choose. What is our heart's delight? When we feel the excitement of the vision, and see clearly the good work, we must step back and ask ourselves, "Yes, but is this *my* work to do?" Perhaps my work is to just hold the vision. Perhaps it is to speak about it or write about it. Perhaps it is to cheer on someone else who may have the means to carry it out.

Letting Go of the Primacy of the Individual

Paradoxically, when we have identified our own sacred work, it allows us to hold all the other work we do in partnership with others more lightly. As we come together in coalitions and groups to bring forth the *collective* work of the New Story, we let go of the story being "my" story, the process being "my" process, the idea being "my" idea, the vision being "my" vision. We don't need to control or take responsibility for the whole thing, and this can be a relief. Ultimately, this frees us up to focus on what we love, to nurture our part, to express our unique gifts, and to know that that is enough and is all that is called for. We don't need to become workaholics in order to help save the world.

Turning Jealousy into Gratitude

The most important thing we can do to be effective in bringing about a new world of joy and self-fulfillment is to deeply appreciate ourselves. How can we honor ourselves, feel the divine "enoughness" of who we are? As we find our fulfilling mission, we can be available to others without a feeling of jealousy, competition, or inner neediness. We are finding our sovereignty, our solidness as powerful beings with a unique and worthy purpose.

One of the things that let me know I was coming out of the Never Enough fog was when I began to be able to use twinges of jealousy as spotlights to look at how I either was or was not taking responsibility for claiming my own Enough Story. Eventually, I was able to inwardly bless and thank people for pointing me in the direction I needed to fine-tune my own work. Once I started to do this, jealousy no longer showed up as my experience. What appeared instead was admiration and gratitude. Everyone becomes your teacher, letting you know what you want to create and what you do not.

Jealousy is often based on a story we are telling ourselves that isn't actually true. Rarely is the fairytale interpretation we may have of another's success an accurate picture. We cannot possibly take in the fullness of what that person has had to sacrifice in order to achieve his or her goals or what hidden burdens came with those achievements. I think we would be a better world if people in the limelight shared the true reality behind the scenes, the downside of achieving success. They probably don't want to seem ungrateful, but it would help us to gain a more accurate picture if they did. I was impressed, for example, when the twenty-one-year-old 2015 Master's champion Jordan Spieth so honestly expressed his trepidation at having reached his lifelong goal of being the best golfer much earlier in his career than he expected to. You could feel his authenticity and vulnerability as he wondered aloud, "Now I have to rethink what to do with the rest of my life."

Pulling Out of Old Relationship Patterns

There is a less obvious form of social ranking that might need to be confronted as well—one I had not realized I was doing. I had an old friend who always came to me with crisis after crisis. She often joked that I was her free therapist. Our talks had always been deep and meaningful, but they sometimes siphoned off a great deal of my time and energy. I stood by her side through her divorce and several job and relationship changes. I wanted to support her and thought I was helping.

Then, one day, I realized with some discomfort that I had tended to attract the kind of friendship where I could play the role of the counselor. I hadn't ever seen what an ego trip I had been on. I had convinced myself that I was a selfless, compassionate, and patient friend. When I looked at my friendship, I could see that my role had probably actually helped her to stay stuck. I had become her valve for releasing pressure whenever the consequences of her choices felt too painful. Although I had intended to, I had not helped her to find her power. It was a form of the old, disempowering perpetrator-hero-victim story, and I had taken the only desirable role in the scenario, that of the supposed hero. Knowing that, I could not in good conscience continue our pattern. With more integrity and self-awareness than I had ever mustered before, I set some new boundaries that felt healthier. My friend's reaction to the change was swift and full of rage, and I lost her permanently as a friend.

We are each responsible for claiming our own sovereignty. Whether it is establishing healthy boundaries or renegotiating patterns of behavior that don't ultimately serve in the way we had intended, a Sovereign takes personal responsibility for herself and wishes no harm toward others. It is ironic, but when I asked my friend for some new boundaries, I was treating her with more respect and I was feeling more understanding and compassion for her than ever. I cared enough to not participate in recycling the same patterns of suffering.

You cannot expect to be understood or regarded well for making such a choice. But by somehow knowing in my heart that I was doing the least harm this way I could find inner peace about it, a feeling of having ultimately done the right thing even if on the surface it may have looked like rejection. We participate in all sorts of Never Enough dramas as victims, dependents, energy grabbers, energy leakers, martyrs, perpetrators, and heroes. We have written ourselves and others into stories that repeat old painful patterns. The journey from Never Enough to Enough involves bringing these stories into the light of awareness to be dissolved and healed. How do we participate in creating unnecessary suffering for others? In what ways do we accept roles that create unnecessary suffering for ourselves? As we do this important and challenging inner work, we lighten ourselves, attracting new patterns that do not involve suffering. As we pull out of old dramas, we lessen the number of traps set in the world for people to fall into. We free ourselves and others to create Enough.

Overcoming the Fear of Loneliness and Rejection

There will be those who will not understand your Enough perspective and who will not move with you as you step into more clarity and empowerment. And although this is scary and sad, this does not mean you should hold back your process. New people will start to show up in your life to guide you and to keep you company along the way. You will not be alone in the new territory. The world needs us to become our sovereign selves, grounded, purposeful, clear, possessed of our full energy, and unapologetic for it. This is the only way we have the vitality and clarity to move into the New Story, to establish sanctuary for everyone there.

This calls on us to have a new definition of compassion. In the case of my friendship, it was ultimately compassionate to both of us to break the cycle of our dysfunctional friendship. Everyone has her or his own sacred work to do to reclaim wholeness. I honor my friend's sacred journey. I don't need to fix her. I don't need to energetically meet her in misery, either. I have my own sacred work to do. I can simply send her love and wish her grace and ease. I can leave the door open for our friendship to meet in a higher vibe. Maybe she will and maybe she won't join me again, but it is infringing on her sovereignty to impose my expectations or judgments on her. That is just me trying to control the world rather than accepting what is. The rejection of what is is what creates suffering. We serve the greater good best when we align with what is true for us by honoring our freedom to channel our energy however and wherever we choose.

The needs in the world are many. It is easy to lose our focus by stretching ourselves too thin and by neglecting our own self-care. But we are being called on now to be absolutely steadfast and courageous in reserving energy to do the work that calls to us most deeply right now. As ironic as it may seem in a Share to Transform culture, certain boundaries right now are our friends. *The trick is to have boundaries while keeping our hearts open.* The old world is crumbling loudly all around us. We must remain at the calm eye in the center of the storm and not get drawn into the chaos. Many of us are so used to drama and chaos that we will find it uncomfortable to break free of it. But when we understand that our addiction to drama actually pulls away our power and fragments our energy, we realize that reclaiming ourselves is necessary to build up the resilience and inner coherence we need to serve as emissaries for peace.

We are being asked to focus our intention with more skill than ever before so something more peaceful and grounded can be anchored into Earth. Anything that makes us feel grounded, mindful, focused, and calm is highly beneficial right now. We will reap the greatest outcomes to share with others by staying in the calm center of our being as much as possible. As we impeccably honor our sacred purpose at this critical time on Earth, we establish a new world fit to be inhabited by future generations. This simply isn't the time for miring ourselves in old dramas and outdated roles. We must get down to the business of building the new world. There is no need to leak any energy on anything that does not lead to the unfurling of the New Story. We are here to become the change.

General Periodicity of the "We"

You will recall the progression represented by the geese story and the starling story, how sharing becomes more blended, more synchronous, more graceful as we move from the way geese share to the way starlings share. You will recall how humans as holons have gained a great deal of experience of individual nature over the past five thousand years, and are drawn now to experience what it means to be a member of a connected whole.

When we follow the steady evolution of human consciousness itself, there is a clear directional pattern that moves from a state of separation to ever broader and more intimate affiliations between people, groups, and living beings. This trend can be represented by the GRST timeline, which shows the emergence of progressively more connected forms of human social organization over the centuries. First, the primary form affiliation took was that of family-tribes and then later villages, city-states, and now countries and unions of countries, such as the EU. Some consider the first wave of a global level of affiliation as having been seeded in the collective conscious when *The Blue Marble* photograph of Earth was shared from *Apollo 17* in 1972.

Place the individual and collective growth stories side by side and what you see is a progression in the capacity of human beings and whole cultures to widen their circle of affiliation through time. In other words, to embrace a wider "we."

In table form, it would look like this:

GATHER	REPEAT	SHARE	TRANSFORM
Infant	Child	Adolescent	Adult
Family	Tribe/Village/ Religion/ Political Party	Country	World

←— *Current Range* —→

The light gray area represents the range of human consciousness present on Earth today, with some individuals reflecting a Repeat consciousness (focused on what would be best for my tribe, religion, race, or political party), some reflecting a Share consciousness (focused on what would be best for my community, region, or country), and some reflecting a Transform consciousness (focused on what would be best for the planet). Even though there is a range, collectively our most visible systems—economic, legal, and political—express only a narrow range, represented by the dark gray band. Nonetheless, many very important systems lag well behind this line. For example, some religions and political parties operate largely at the Repeat (tribal) level, seeking a world that conforms to one idea of right and wrong. As we move into the Share range, tolerance of differences and appreciation of diversity become the norm. Theoretically, the tipping point for a new global culture would take place when a critical number of people on Earth embrace a global perspective.

The challenge for those whose consciousness has evolved beyond the mainstream cultural norm is not to get discouraged, but to realize that they can contribute something very valuable simply by demonstrating what is possible and real at their level of understanding. Inherent in the maturation process of consciousness is the capability to expand one's heart, essentially identifying with and communing with a larger and more diverse group of people and living beings. Inherent in the process is the ability to be more peaceful, benevolent, and unconditionally loving. It would be important to find others who share your global perspective, especially to provide validation, synergy, companionship, and support. Even though we experience more meaningful lives as our consciousness expands, it isn't easy to be out of sync with mainstream society. You will surely be ignored or misunderstood by many. Some people may even fear you. But so, too, will you provide living proof of what is possible. Those who are waking up will be inspired by you. For this reason, the most valuable thing we could do is to dare to be our authentic selves even when it would be much easier to try to blend in.

Why is this so important? The GRST model predicts that it is inevitable that humanity will eventually embrace an ability to think globally and therefore will want Enough not only for themselves and their tribe, but for the world. The human developmental and cultural stories are converging to bring forth new potentials we have never seen before, a new passion and capacity to care and respond to multiple crises at a global scale: climate change, poverty, war, and ecosystem destruction. When we shift into an Enough worldview, we naturally take on a long-term focus, a systems perspective, a sense of responsibility to others and a desire to have a positive impact on the well-being of future generations. We are automatically given more energy, motivation, and confidence to make a difference.

In the near future, we will finally understand that we are enhanced not by competing but by cooperating and advancing together. *Together we rise!* The birth of an Enough perspective is as natural and as reliable as adulthood following adolescence. We can count on it. We can be sure that we and future generations will seek these opportunities as much as they seek us.

Enough for everyone is the promise that awaits us on the evolutionary path, a result of doing our inner work to integrate the lessons of Share within ourselves as individuals. We let go of separation and allow ourselves to trust the group process to unfold to our mutual benefit. When we all have our eyes on the well-being of the group, none of us needs to waste our time or energy on self-protectionism. Imagine, for example, a world without the need for a military. From the global (Transform) perspective, nothing could seem as ridiculous as spending billions of dollars to ensure a ready cache of bombs aimed at one another "just in case." When we move into the Transform era, energy spent on self-defense is freed up to invest in building better social systems that serve the common good, providing for basic needs such as clean water, clean air, shelter, and food that never should have been preempted by militarism in the first place.

Labels Limit

We are being asked at this time of global shift to drop into our hearts and into our greatest wishes for the world. Can we realistically accomplish these wishes on our own? I really don't see how. When we move beyond tribalism and touch our essence, we access something we've never fully experienced before, the power of true collective resonance. As we move into an internal sense of "I am enough," any labels we previously used to demark people as different from us lose their meaning. We recognize labels as mere symbols, as useful shorthand to represent and coalesce ideas, not as boxes that define us or have the power to override our underlying unity. Labels cannot possibly convey the wholeness of who you are or what you dream. When we are welcomed and seen as our whole, essential selves, labels lose their power to divide.

I was recently hosting an Enough telecircle for a group of very spiritually open and aware women. Our conversations lived mostly in Transform territory. One of the women in our group came forward to share an issue about a relative. He was a public figure and had been interviewed by her local news channel speaking out against the children coming over the border from Mexico. His stance was rife with racial hatred, blame, and division. She shared her exasperation with us. "I am afraid at our next family gathering that I am going to blow up at him. Every time he is interviewed by the media and he spouts hatred, I want to scream. He goes against everything I believe in."

This woman took a significant risk being the first in our group to inject such unsettling emotions into the circle, which usually centered around topics of unity, love, acceptance, and tolerance. I admired her courage in allowing herself to be vulnerable in this way. I knew that her issue reflected a challenge I knew well, one shared by those of us who are striving to embody Enough while living in a world seemingly dominated by Never Enoughers. What do we do when we rub up against someone who is coming from a consciousness of scarcity? As she spoke, an image appeared in my head that I thought might be very comforting as well as instructive for all of us who can relate to her situation.

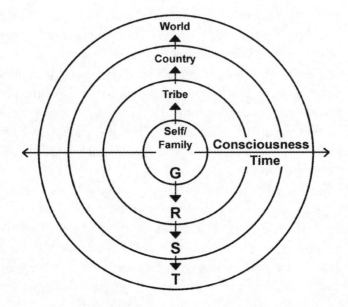

Enough!

Think of the image on the previous page as the ripples created by dropping a stone in a pond. Ripples expand out from the center as a function of time. Now think of these ripples as representing the expansion of human consciousness through time. Each ripple represents humanity reaching a new, more expansive stage of what I call "affiliative consciousness." Affiliative consciousness is how much "other" we can identify with as a "we."

For example, we begin as babies learning that we are an independent self. As we grow older, we realize we are part of a group called a family (represented by G for Gather).

As we become aware of our broader neighborhood and community, we realize we are also members of various other groups who share something in common with us, such as our age, religion, philosophy, language, or race (represented by R for Repeat).

As we learn about the larger world through school, books, and the media, we understand that we are citizens of a country and that our country is made up of people whose various races, religions, political views, and philosophies do not necessarily mirror our own (represented by S for Share). Share is actually a big leap in consciousness, because it is at this point that we realize affiliation does not require nearly as much visible, outward evidence of sameness as it did in the Repeat stage of development. At Share, we are looking beyond what we can see, hear, touch, and feel and are tuning in to something more subtle yet enduring which is unitive—what makes us a human family. For example, the United States is founded on ideas of liberty, equality, and democracy for all.

As a collective world society, we have only scratched the surface of Share and still have a way to go to fully integrate Share consciousness. The ripple model would suggest that by the time we reach the Transform ripple (represented by T), it means we have internally integrated the understanding that we are *global* citizens, sharing an awareness of our *common humanity* and *common fate* with all other human beings, and eventually, as we move through Transform, with all living beings on Earth. Indeed, the leading edge of Transform consciousness is what we see happening through many individuals and groups right now!

So what are we to do if our consciousness has expanded into Transform territory but we must still live and work in a world that is reflecting mostly Repeat and Share? It may be helpful to know that each ripple both includes and transcends the previous ripples. We don't unlearn or negate what we learned in previous stages of consciousness; those smaller ripples just cease to be our primary identity. For example, I am at the same time a family member, a member of the community, a citizen of my country, and a global citizen. When I am writing this book, I am coming mostly from the perspective of a global citizen. I know that a global perspective will benefit my country, community, and family because as a global citizen, I understand everything on Earth is intricately interdependent and interconnected. This does not work in reverse. If all I am focused on is protecting the best interests of my family, I could possibly harm the community, my country, or the world and not even know it. When my interests are narrow, I cannot see these wider impacts and therefore am not able to take responsibility for them. The wider my perspective, the more likely my actions will be aligned with the greater good.

While in various situations I will make decisions based on G (family), R (tribe), S (country), or T (world), but once I reach an awareness that I am a global citizen (T), it changes how I interact overall. It changes what I value. It changes how open I dare to keep my heart. It changes what emotions I access and how I interpret the world around me. We cannot understand a bigger ripple until we have experienced it personally ourselves. What this means is that we cannot expect someone whose primary consciousness is Repeat (their tribe), like the relative of the woman in my circle, to be able to understand or be influenced by logic or values that come from a wider Transform perspective. It quite literally is a language gap between two different worldviews. What is effective in this case? Compassion and detachment. What do compassion and detachment look like in this situation?

We remember that the primary purpose of Repeat is to replicate one worldview. Change and growth are not sought out or desired. What is desired is an orderly society that operates under one set of rigid, never-changing rules in which an authority figure such as a parent, dictator, or religious leader keeps everyone in line. The assumption is that people are not capable of managing their own moral and behavioral direction so need rules and authority figures to guide them. The sharing of new and different ideas is seen as a threat to this orderly arrangement. From a Repeat consciousness, Enough for everyone can never be achieved. It simply isn't the goal. Spreading sameness is, even if sameness stands in the way of anyone ever getting his or her specific Enough. Freedom, self-expression, and diversity of perspectives are unwelcome. The evolutionary flow that brings expanded consciousness is seen as a threat to one's perceived safe, orderly world.

If someone cannot embrace change to their one-size-fits-all world, such as an influx of immigrants or a different religious or political perspective, it does no good to label that person wrong, even if we know in our hearts it is. It is more productive to understand that the person is suffering from a Never Enough mindset that keeps him or her in fear and scarcity. In the case of my telecircle friend, if her relative's affiliation goes only as far as "citizen of the USA," he probably perceives illegal immigrants as a threat to him and to his country's sovereignty. Most likely, though, the real fear comes from thinking that immigrants do not share his values, customs, or way of life, and therefore that his and his family's way of life is under direct threat. By labeling them "other," he feels he can justify regarding them not as fellow human beings but as criminals, welfare recipients, or drug dealers. That is Repeat consciousness. My telecircle friend is doing the opposite, relating to the immigrants from the common humanity she shares with them. She may have recalled that members of her own family were once also immigrants to the United States. She can empathize with immigrants about the suffering and stress that goes along with a journey into a foreign land, not speaking the language or knowing the customs or laws. My friend has applied her expanded affiliative consciousness to several volunteer jobs helping to empower women, including incarcerated women.

One of the most primal needs human beings have is safety. When our fears rule our behavior, we are highly vulnerable to extremist solutions, despots, isolationism, impulsiveness, violence, and the erosion of freedoms and civil liberties. When fear rules our behavior, we close off our hearts not only from the "scary world" outside, but also from ourselves. The price is to keep tribalism and hatred, hallmarks of a Never Enough culture, alive.

It may seem at times as though the world is going backwards, that division is on the rise. Media bias against reporting good news will certainly make it seem that way. Our learned addiction to drama and conflict will also make it seem that way. As understandable as it is for someone's narrower viewpoint to make us feel angry or concerned that the hatred will spread, perhaps we can gain some sense of comfort that narrower thinking is no match to the steady expansion of consciousness that is happening on Earth, as recent changes in attitudes about marijuana and gay and transgendered rights have revealed. This trend toward embracing more diversity and freedom of choice cannot be stopped. A rise in something old often means a final clearing of it. And as we have seen, nature's pattern never goes in the direction of T S R G. We are loving ourselves and one another more and better all the time. We are steadily moving through Share and into Transform, both individually and collectively. We are daring to reach out, connecting and trusting across differences and learning that together we are, in fact, stronger, safer, and more resilient when we do so. This is not aberrant behavior exhibited by a small number of hippies, "liberal crazies," free thinkers, cultural creatives, or New Agers. It is humanity's evolutionary growing edge showing itself more and more. The expansion of affiliative consciousness is an opportunity, not a threat. It is an opportunity to access more skills for achieving global, local, and individual healing and peace. Our response should not be to huddle in fear but to welcome this expansion with open arms.

When we encounter hatred and division, we can take this as our signal to move resolutely out to the next ripple, which embraces everything with far more love and compassion. We can let go of needing the world to be perfect and harmonious right away. We can let go of feeling responsible for righting every wrong we witness. We can take strength in knowing that the flow of history is firmly on the side of love and unity. It is a sacred and divine process, providing timely lessons for each individual soul, and you are the proof of it. The future belongs to those who bring in a broader, more loving perspective than the mainstream currently offers. It has always been this way. Minute by minute, without you needing to do anything about it other than to love and respect yourself, fear-based consciousness is losing its power to control the world.

Blurring Boundaries

America is a rich melting pot culture that epitomizes Share. However, even within our borders there are limits on how much diversity is welcome. Capitalist principles that vie for a place within our democracy are still rooted in Repeat, or survival of the fittest mentality. Though America is supposed to be a country whose government is of, by, and for the people, there is still a significant struggle between individualism and group welfare. We see this played out in the battles between Republicans (who tend to believe in the primacy of the individual) and Democrats (who tend to believe in the primacy of the group).

The boundaries between "other" and "self," which were crystal clear in the Repeat phase (*my* kin, *my* religion, *my* village, *my* sports team, *my* race), start to blur in the Share phase. Often mistaken for "a weakening in the moral fiber of society," greater diversity can awaken insecurity and fear in people if they don't understand that this blurring is actually progress. When we are afraid, we tend to revert to the simplicity and either/or thinking of the Repeat. For example, when our affiliation is country but we don't like the president's policies, we tend to revert to Repeat affiliations such as "conservative" or "progressive" in order to recover our sense of power and security.

The blurring in the Share explains why it feels like we are living in an increasingly confusing and chaotic world. The boundaries we thought were so essential to understanding the world and to ensuring our safety are not as real or solid as we once thought. Words such as "capitalism" and "democracy" no longer take on a squeaky-clean, black-and-white connotation. We recognize the gray areas, the pervasive threads of abuse and corruption, but also the good intentions that run through both sides of any endeavor. We are confronted with the paradox that perhaps it isn't either/or but both/and. We can look at the confusion and complexity as proof of progress: *The dissolving of "otherness" is exactly what the evolution of consciousness intends for us.* If we realize this, we can begin to get excited that we are right where we should be in the process. The Transform/adult phase of humanity is just around the corner.

Choosing Our Story

Just because evidence of Enough doesn't appear regularly in the nightly news doesn't mean it isn't already present on a grand scale on Earth. The vein of Enough running through the human story has been strong and vibrant, an unbroken flow going back to the beginning of time. So to join in the effort to improve the world, we don't ever need to start from scratch or go it alone. All we need to do is connect our own passion and gifts to this enduring undercurrent, flow with what has already been done, and feel the kinship and power of the countless hearts who have shared the very same visions and dreams we hold in our own hearts today.

The stories we tell ourselves matter, so it serves us to be conscious of which stories we choose to tell and how we tell them. What we need is more encouragement for people to boldly tell their Enough stories. *Kosmos Journal* and *YES! Magazine* are sources I look to for this kind of news. It is motivating to hear how people are gathering together to make a better world. It creates a sense that we too can join that wave of joyful doing. There is much worthy work to be done. Many are doing it with a sense of joyful engagement and anticipation, trusting that when they engage in building to fulfill their ideals, there will be fewer victims and more hands on deck.

⌒ 8 ⌒

We Have Enough

*By pooling our talents, power, passions, and resources, we
ensure our security and exponentialize our capacity to create
a world that works for everyone.*

*There is one thing which America demonstrates invincibly, and
of which I had been in doubt up till now: it is that the middle classes can
govern a state. . . . In spite of their petty passions, their incomplete
education and their vulgar manners, they clearly can provide practical
intelligence, and that is found to be enough.*
—Alexis de Tocqueville

The future belongs to those who believe in the beauty of their dreams.
—Eleanor Roosevelt

As we make the leap from me to we, how do we know we are building our lives on solid and fertile ground, and not investing in some rosy illusion or some impractical New Age dream? Not to worry. Grassroots proof is flooding in from all over the globe that this transformation is real and that it is producing practical results. What follows is just a brief snapshot of the exciting Enough Story that is blossoming all over the globe. As you sense the monumental scale of what is happening in our midst, I believe your "Enough detector" will be turned on. You will discover for yourself more proof in your community, online, and everywhere you look.

Paul Hawken's book *Blessed Unrest* provided for the first time a sense of the truly monumental scale of grassroots change, the organic and independent arising of multiple movements across the globe. He concluded that not only do these add up to the biggest citizen-led movement the world has ever seen, but these movements comprise "nature's immune response" to the sick paradigm in which we live. We can trust this impulse implicitly because it comes from a common place inside us that feels Earth's pain as our own. But it also comes from a place that taps Earth's healing wisdom as our own.

Building an Enough World is exceedingly difficult work. As we "live into" Enough values and insights more fully, we tend to notice that the old templates for how to work collectively do not fit. At the same time we are creating new Enough projects and products, we must face the additional challenge of inventing new ways of working together. It is often the case in this rushed, task-oriented world that we unconsciously, or in the name of expediency, default back to old models of organization such as hierarchies. When we find these old ways of organizing cannot possibly lead to Enough outcomes, we may give up too quickly on our new projects. But if we keep trying, we will build a body of knowledge about what social structures *do* lead to New Story success. As we consciously work with Enough principles, we enter an unprecedented age of social reinvention. Many in the fields of psychology, sociology, education, anthropology, politics, law, and economics will feel drawn to providing new social guideposts for humanity.

Letting Go so the New Story Can Emerge

I recently had the opportunity to observe a live stream of the New Story Summit. This multiday conference, hosted by the preeminent intentional community, Findhorn, gathered some of the world's most innovative thinkers, artists, healers, and change agents to work on gaining a better understanding of the emerging New Story for humanity and Earth.

The organizers had clearly worked very consciously to design and implement a format that would be rooted in Enough principles of equality, democracy, and co-creativity. They beautifully blended in visual and performing arts. They balanced inspiring keynote addresses with spontaneously formed workshops and action teams. They included ceremony and surprise. It was impressive.

The core of the conference was an opportunity for those present to self-organize into groups. These groups were led by participants, not by preselected workshop presenters, using a method known as Open Space Technology. Open Space is a process developed by Harrison Owen with four basic tenets: "Whoever comes is the right people. Whatever happens is the only thing that could have. Whenever it starts is the right time. When it is over, it is over."

Open Space is an intrinsically uncomfortable process for many people because it requires deep trust, not only in one another, but also in the reliability of self-organization to lead to desirable outcomes. Built into the Open Space methodology is the Enough idea that we are all driven by a universal impulse or heart-knowing that will guide us rightly. For the process to work, we must learn to trust this bigger impulse. This is where feminine qualities such as patience, allowing, letting go, and nonjudgment come in as primary virtues for anyone who is co-creating the New Story.

Partway through the New Story Summit there was a mini coup. In the middle of the night, some of the participants had hijacked the boards on which the spontaneous work sessions had been posted, spelling out "We don't know" in Post-it notes. It had come after an uncomfortable period of dissention. As far as I could discern (and this is probably oversimplifying the reality of what actually happened), some people had come to the conference with the expectation that they would meet others joining them in anger and frustration toward the 1 percent. Some needed to find support and a safe space to deeply grieve all the suffering perpetuated on living beings and Earth. Others came ready to jump into creating coalitions for action and had no patience for emotional processing. On top of this, the participatory design of the conference meant that the flow was often energetically jarring and at the mercy of whoever came forward in the moment to speak into the microphone. Some speakers came to the microphone with a mature awareness of the balance between their own need to be heard with the needs and the flow of the larger group. Others, for a variety of reasons, felt justified in disregarding collective considerations in favor of their own sense of rightness and timing.

Even as a silent observer from afar, I felt my own impatience and judgment flair at times, and then I needed to look at my reaction and ask if any of my own expectations or needs took precedence over anyone else's. The answer was, of course not. We are co-evolving together as a larger system, and this calls upon us to cultivate more compassion and patience than we ever have before. The world needs those with righteous indignation, those who feel Earth's pain, and those ready to take action. Entering this larger melting pot of perceiving and expectation can make us feel very vulnerable and uncomfortable, particularly when we have been reared to create safety and predictability by ordering the world with labels such as religion, political party, race, age, gender, and cultural and educational background.

Patience and Practice

What I have found is that Never Enough separation stands in the way of us perceiving the bonds that are always there. Never Enough also prevents us from leveraging those bonds of unity into some kind of collectively powerful action. It is the old disempowering "divide and conquer" methodology of the Never Enough culture, and we must question it wherever we find it, particularly within ourselves. This means we may temporarily feel more vulnerable and out of control than ever. But the truth is that we are never more vulnerable and powerless as when we are divided against one another. The control we've been told we have as an independent individual in the big system is in large part an illusion. Isn't it time that we understand our strength, our ace in the hole, is in standing together for common values and common visions? Finding a new level of collective coherence takes time, patience, spiritual maturity, and yes, quite a bit of messy, chaotic practice. Entering a phase of practicing (and tolerating doing it badly at first) is absolutely necessary to planetary transformation. We are on the move to a new, lighter, more graceful way of being.

Living the Questions

In order to create something new, we need to be open to new ideas, new information, and new perceptions about what works and what is possible. I have found this kind of inner openness and humbleness to be highly beneficial to my own growth. My favorite graduate school professor used to call this state of being "living the questions." Welcoming a state of "living the questions" prevents us from letting in the unwanted guests of self-righteous ego (when we feel certain we know) and shame (when we feel pretty certain that we do not know). Living the questions opens our hearts and minds to discovering something new and hopefully better. We are saying yes to the teachable moment in which we give up trying to be or know it all. We take on beginner's mind. And when we enter this state of mind, everyone in the room shines with the potentiality of being our teachers, whether we agree or disagree with them.

We learn from those holding anger how to access our own sacred indignation, the fire in our bellies to fuel action. We learn from mourners how to acknowledge our own sadness for the world's pain and how to trust enough to both receive and give healing comfort in an intimate and vulnerable way, affirming our bonds of trust and humanity. We learn from planners that we collectively do have the skills, intellect, and collective will to rebuild the world. All of it is okay. All of it is, in fact, absolutely, beautifully necessary. What isn't necessary is clinging to the old ways of doing things that are steeped in rigidity, judgment, competition, and fear, the idea that we must come to consensus on one way forward when in fact what we really need is the kind of solid underlying unity that includes and allows the diversity of many ways. What isn't necessary is pretending we're not feeling vulnerable, afraid, angry, sad, or impatient. Of course we are! We are in a time between planetary stories. All of these emotions can draw us forward into new understandings, but only as long as we remain open to them.

Circle Leadership

One particularly powerful form of building new understandings within ourselves and with others is circle technology. Based on indigenous practices of tribal council, the circle is what Christina Baldwin and Ann Linnea, coauthors of *The Circle Way*, called "the first and future" form of human organization. Lost to us when hierarchy became the dominant form of human organization, circle nevertheless perpetually resonates as a foundational way to foster community. Who isn't drawn to gathering around a campfire? Who hasn't felt the sense of belonging that comes from standing in circle, hand in hand, singing a common song?

A wisdom circle is characterized by engaging with others in deep listening and self-reflection. There is usually something, such as a vase of flowers or a candle in the middle, to symbolize our common grounding in essence, something commonly referred to as the circle's sacred center, with each of us seated like spokes of a wheel around that center.

Through circle, we honor our own journey of becoming and we practice noninterference in others' journey of becoming. We do this by extending deep listening to others and by sharing our authentic emotions, values, struggles, and dreams. When first learning the circle way, we tend to need to be shown how to listen deeply. We have been used to listening conditionally, formulating our opinion or response while the other person is still speaking. Deep listening means giving our full attention to what we are hearing, and doing so from a place of compassion, not judgment. A talking piece is often used to remind people to not default to two-way conversation, advice giving, or interrupting. The person with the talking piece is the only one who speaks. Each person has the opportunity to be the holder of the talking piece and to receive deep listening from the rest of the group.

What happens over time within a wisdom circle is that the stories tend to find some kind of common ground, coherence, theme, or pattern as the talking stick goes around the circle. That theme could be letting go, embracing change, feeling stuck, learning to say no, grieving, taking a leap of faith. As miraculous as it seems, everyone leaves refreshed and supported without any kind of coaching, advice, or direct help being offered. The individual retains her autonomy, her timing, and her process, and feels safe to share intimate emotions and issues. What we end up cultivating in circle is trust, wisdom, and compassion for ourselves and others.

My interest in circles took me to the United Nations Commission on the Status of Women in 2013 and 2014, where I helped to convene a group of nongovernmental organizations who share a common interest in circle methodology. As simple as circle is, many consider it the most promising method for cultivating peace, democracy, cross-cultural understanding, and equality in the world today. Far from fluff, I believe circle is absolutely foundational to the New Story of peace and intercultural harmony.

The Sovereign Contractor

The wisdom circle gives us an idea of "right balance" between the needs of individual and group, inner and outer, but when it comes to taking concrete action, how do we honor our individual mission within the dynamics of a larger group? When we have been so indoctrinated into competing, how do we trust others to have the best intentions for supporting our sacred ideas and projects? When I helped to form Imagine the Good Foundation, we introduced the role of sovereign contractor in response to these questions. The sovereign contractor (SC) is an individual with a project idea or passion who affiliates with a cooperative group or organization for support. By coming to a circle of colleagues, the SC has the opportunity to be received first and foremost as a whole person rather than primarily as an employee whose work is at the service of a company. Each member of the group is responsible for implementation of his or her own ideas, but anyone can ask the group for help, feedback, ideas, resources, contacts, and expertise. Cost savings can be realized when the circle of SCs share office space, office equipment, and legal, accounting, and marketing help. SCs engage in Enough reciprocity by the principle of paying it forward and giving back to their colleagues and to the supporting organization itself.

Coworking

Coworking is a larger trend that arose as a solution to the isolation people experience when working independently at home. In 2005, Brad Neuberg opened the first coworking site in San Francisco. Since then, the number of coworking office spaces has roughly doubled each year. Coworkers not only share office space but also enjoy many other benefits. Coworking gives people access to ongoing social and professional support and a communal space to connect and discuss and hone ideas.

A natural benefit of groups of sovereign contractors or coworkers is that we are exchanging something of value with one another, but these exchanges need not involve money or competition. Each time we exchange, we are experiencing our enoughness, or how our gifts meet the world's great need. We are learning to receive, trusting our needs will be met with the willing gifts and generosity of others. And we are abiding by the Enough mantra, "Together we rise!"

The Sharing Economy

While the sovereign contractor is a way to exchange services and support within a new kind of business organization, there are myriad ways communities are reviving this concept as a new economic model, sharing tools, sharing space, trading hours, and forming cooperatives. The sharing movement includes all of these and more.

I recently sat down with my dear friend, Linda Hogan, cofounder of hOurworld, an international training and software cooperative that supports all kinds of community currency exchanges. Community currency is the general term used to refer to a variety of exchanges such as food co-ops, buy local movements, and service exchanges. Linda's lifelong passion has been to help people share "relationship currency," exchanging care and compassion with neighbors. The idea is that we "re-village" our communities, strengthening local support systems and the meaningfulness, interconnectedness, and resiliency that go along with it.

Members of a service exchange sign up to provide and receive any kind of service they wish, such as pet sitting, gardening, baking, or home repair. Many professionals have joined the exchange, offering services from accounting to health care to counseling to massage to computer repair.

A key element of a service exchange is the idea that all people in the exchange are equal. An hour of my time is worth an hour of your time no matter what service we each offer. Hours are earned whenever a service is provided. This hour can be "spent" to obtain services from anyone else in the exchange. Linda's hope is that once these networks of exchanges become a regular part of our lives, we make authentic connections with our neighbors and eventually we will not need formalized service exchanges. We become relationship currency in action.

The community currency movement is a tangible demonstration that "We have Enough," encouraging us to expand our idea of what comprises wealth and worth. When we look at ourselves and recognize the broader selection of skills and expertise we are able to offer to others, we realize we are wealthier and more valuable than we realized. Turning these skills into exchanges not only validates our sense of "having enough" to give, but in "being enough" to be deserving of receiving what it is we need. What we discover is that we get so much more—a recovered sense of belonging, meaning, and community. We have increased our wealth beyond what we could have imagined.

When I first started writing about Enough, the sharing economy was just starting to be widely visible to the mainstream. Since then, commerce has found it could not ignore this growing trend. It has seeped into almost every aspect of life—how we vacation, how we donate to charities, how we eat, how we shop, how we educate ourselves. Homegrown efforts such as buy local, flash mobs, resilience hubs, Transition Towns, and farm co-ops are popping up everywhere. The spontaneous creativity and hybridization are amazing, such as flash mobs for gardening known as permablitzing, or the idea of meditation flash mobs, known as MedMobs. Our creativity is expanding beyond the tight mental models of scarcity economics. Add to that the growing realization that the world economy is in fact a debt-based system, a Ponzi scheme by which no wealth is created without a larger and corresponding debt burden, and it is no surprise that people are exercising their freedom to give and receive freely and locally, as Earth has always done.

The False Sharing Economy

As we move into human murmuration, we are discovering that we naturally apply greater discernment to everything we encounter, weeding out the true Enough Story from the imitation Enough Story. Discernment is sensing the intentions behind something. Discernment is noticing the real substance that is beneath the shiny outer trappings. Once you know to look deeper, discerning the real truth is easy. There is always proof in plain sight to confirm what the core intention behind an endeavor may be.

Enough is a very simple litmus test. Does it provide enough for individuals, communities, *and* Earth? Does it pay it forward *and* give back? Some of the more highly publicized sharing economy platforms fail the Enough test. Airbnb is one example. Airbnb is an online service that matches rooms and homes for rent with short-term guests for a fee. The cofounders of Airbnb were touted as brilliant entrepreneurs for attracting billions in venture capital for their online company. Meanwhile, those doing the sharing on this platform do not share in any part of that venture capital. Uber, the ride-sharing platform, is another example of a sharing economy business that's not ideal. It has been accused of exploiting people by offering them the same work as a taxi driver, but without any of the security or benefits. Both Uber and Airbnb are being scrutinized for negatively impacting the most vulnerable in our society. These new businesses redistribute wealth to those who already have more than enough while shrinking the number of jobs for the least fortunate, such as those who need jobs as chambermaids, hotel laundry workers, and taxi and shuttle drivers in order to survive. In addition, when all a business has done is monetize something that used to be offered for free to friends, extended family, and neighbors, it is actually cutting into the free flow of kindness and support that formed the backbone of community. How is this paying it forward? How is this giving back?

Companies like Google and Facebook have found a way to profit from our impulse to share with one another, luring us to platforms where we can share and network for free, all the while selling our data and helping marketing companies to target us with their pitches. Sharing is an Enough intention, but only if it is not profit-motivated, secretive, or used to harm, exploit, spy on, or control.

Figuring out how to create a win-win-win relationship between the individual, the collective, and the planet is the social architecture challenge of our times. There will be bumps in the road as we figure out the proper balance, but this is where we have and I believe will see the most innovation, aliveness, and engaging action arising in our culture. The new balance will come into focus as we ease into a feeling of enoughness, feeling more trusting as well as more generous as we form new kinds of partnerships and collectives that work for everyone. We are remembering that humans are communal creatures and are happiest when we belong within a lively, interactive, interdependent village where we are treated as precious and equal. As we experience what this feels like, we will more easily be able to discern between the endeavors whose intentions are what they say they are and those that are not.

The Global Commons Movement

A corresponding movement about "the commons" is another indication that we are moving out of the Never Enough economic models of the past. The creative commons openly shares ideas, technologies, creative works, and computer code without requiring payment. For example, one of the fastest-growing video games, Minecraft, was built on the premise that those coming to the game would participate in designing the set in which they played. This idea of player-as-maker has truly exploded. Minecraft fans have taken the invitation to co-create much wider than the sets in which they play, creating YouTube channels where they share videos, contests, and musical parodies. Independent coders create mini games, modifications, and add-ons, while others host unique servers where Minecrafters come to participate in survival games and scavenger hunts.

Another example of player-as-maker is virtual reality technology. Palmer Luckey, the twenty-one-year-old founder of Oculus Rift, made headlines when, to the deep disappointment of his early supporters, he sold his virtual reality headset company to Facebook for $2 billion in March 2014. Prior to the sale, his business model was an inclusive one, open sourcing the original prototype, launching a Kickstarter campaign to produce build-it-yourself VR headsets, and releasing Oculus demonstration kits to amateur game developers and tech enthusiasts. His intention was to encourage them to participate in research and development and to get started on designing games that could symbiotically run on the Rift.

A parallel but much more critical commons movement seeks to gain recognition for the rights of the planet, for the living creatures sharing the planet, and for future generations to thoughtfully share the natural commons such as clean water and clean air. The environmental commons movement seeks to make corporations economically and legally responsible for the damage they do to the commons in the name of short-term profits and seeks to reclaim these common domains from corporate exploitation and control. Obviously, this is a direct and urgent demonstration of the organic impulse to create Enough for self, community, and planet.

Is High Tech Compatible with the Enough Story?

What will saying "Enough is enough!" to the old paradigm of unworthiness, scarcity, and greed look like? Will it be a time of depravity as we pull out of the old systems we've been used to? Will we need to revert to less advanced societies, subsisting on low tech for everything from water to food, shelter, and communication? I imagined that if so, life in my part of the world would get pretty unbearable during the frozen winter months. I felt more than a little resistance to this bleak vision of the future. It didn't feel at all like Enough to me.

But what I see more clearly now is that in an Enough culture, the fulcrum of power must move from multinational companies to local communities. This does not have to mean that the technology companies must go away. What is changing is our relationship with those companies and the rules and ethics by which they are granted permission to have access to our business. In other words, the Enough paradigm will ensure that our consciousness and our spirituality will inform and regulate our technology. It will not eradicate technology.

The Never Enough mindset has bred severe separation— we no longer know our neighbors and communities, and this has been a hugely disempowering dynamic. As individuals, we do not have the power to say no to huge companies. But as the sharing economies take hold, this naturally begins to change. Groups of people will determine their enough as a community and will begin to set the rules by which they will be served by companies that are nonlocal. Access will likely be predicated on the company's ability to demonstrate reciprocity and respect for the environmental commons and for the community. What will be different is not whether or not there will be high technology, but who determines the rules by which companies have access to customers and the commons for labor and materials. Companies who do not honor a commitment to reciprocity and protecting the commons will not gain access to local markets.

A big picture is emerging of people who are in touch with their own enoughness and foster the enoughness of their communities. With the sharing economy as an increasingly common way of life, communities will become much more connected, self-confident, and self-aware about the resources they already have within their citizenry and local area. They will be more resilient and heart-connected, which will greatly improve the quality of life for everyone. Communities may need to be able to demonstrate that they can stand alone to provide the basics for their citizens if need be, but rarely will they actually need to live an isolationist lifestyle as a long-term strategy. That would be the old fear-based self-protectionism and separation of Never Enough. New businesses will demonstrate more cooperative forms, owned and run by the people. Transparency and stewardship will become the key assets any business will need to thrive in the Enough economy.

If it seems impossible that such a shift could really happen, for the people of Feldheim, Germany, it already has. Feldheim is a small village of 145 residents who set a goal to become completely energy independent. Their efforts began in the 1990s when the town installed a single wind turbine to take advantage of the strong winds in the region. Now the town's wind park contains more wind turbines than houses. In 2008, the town built a €1.7 million biogas factory that converts pig manure and unused corn into heat. In 2010, the residents each chipped in €3,000 to build their own electric grid. Feldheim didn't achieve energy independence all at once; it happened gradually, each success leading to further successes. The town next plans to invest in building storage facilities that will hold enough emergency power to meet demand for two days.

The flow toward local sufficiency, like the process in Feldheim, will most likely happen in a gradual and peaceful way. People will feel inspired and connected as they reach each successive goal together. The younger generation, who is used to the player-as-maker dynamic, will naturally create a world in which roles like consumer and provider are more blended. Companies with expertise can either join the creative commons as teachers and models of high tech ways to make this faster and easier, or they can choose to be left behind in the self-sufficiency revolution. Since it is good for business to provide what the customer wants, I believe most of them will choose to join.

The Age of the Workaround

All of the above demonstrate that we are well into the age of the workaround. Where power players such as corporations control the flow of power, money, choice, and energy, we find ways to bypass them by crafting a workaround that makes access to these resources more direct. Lack of access to quality, free education? Along comes Khan Academy, whose motto is "You only have to know one thing: You can learn anything. For free. For everyone. Forever." Fed up with a debt-based monetary system? Along come Bitcoin, Ithaca Hours, and time banking to facilitate person-to-person service exchanges. Have a non-profit idea but don't want to incorporate or have to seek grants? Along come Kickstarter and Indiegogo. You will notice that all of these represent a pattern of peaceful transformation. They do not do direct battle with the powers that be. They simply create workarounds that give people more direct power to determine their futures.

What is so exciting about the age of the workaround is that the workaround is like a leak in a dam. Once we have broken through the old barrier, we are not going back. The flow is one way. The flow of innovation, creativity, and collective synergy is in our favor, and with each drop that is liberated from the dam, the dam itself is weakened. With our newfound discernment, we will be vigilant for corporate lobbying efforts to turn back our freedom to choose, such as the current efforts to challenge net neutrality and allow wholesale spying. Any effort to create unfair advantage; concentrate wealth and power; insulate corporations from being responsible for their negligence, mistakes, or crimes; and anything that keeps people in paranoia or fear will be recognized as the old Never Enough Story fighting for its survival tooth and nail. We can join hand in hand with the confidence of knowing that the evolutionary flow from me to we is real and is moving swiftly within and amongst us as our collective future.

≈ 9 ≈

Enough!

Together we stand in our power to claim a future that is a match to our deepest values.

A miracle worker is not geared toward fighting the world that is, but toward creating the world that could be.

—Marianne Williamson

There is a phrase for this watershed moment of taking back the right we have to change humanity's course, and it comes from a place of incredible power and positivity. It is a triumphant call from the deepest and most sacred part of ourselves that is reclaiming our ability to be the masters of our own destiny. It is the cry, directed at anything that does not ring true, of "Enough is enough!"

Enough! The last line of the Enough Message came as a strong piece of punctuation. It said, "Stand in your power!" It said, "Believe in your truth!" It said, "Let no doubts or fears stand in your way. Trust, act, engage. Don't look back. Look forward, move forward in the direction of your dreams." It said, "Do what you can do. Do what you want to do. It will be enough."

As discussed, the word *enough* is used in many different contexts, and depending on the context can mean different things. But when the word is seen alone, as it is in the last line of the Enough Message, our first impression tends to be to interpret it as expressing disgust or a desire for separation from someone or something. Such a definitive statement certainly carries a bold punch. However, when "Enough is enough!" is our primary orientation toward the word Enough, then we must be careful that we aren't actually expressing separation, or Never Enough. I think for this reason it was no accident that "Enough!" was given as the last sentence of the Enough Message and not the first. I think it is also why it was given as "Enough!" rather than "Enough is enough!" If it came first, we might interpret the message as an instruction to blame and separate instead of to align our efforts to our dreams. When "Enough!" comes at the end of the Enough Message, it serves more as a bon voyage than a proclamation of anger or frustration. It symbolizes a *turning away from* one pattern of life to powerfully, definitively claim a new one, as in "Been there, done that. Now, I'm moving on."

Claiming or Battling

To claim the life you really want is a very significant and positive act. You are trusting yourself, taking responsibility and affirming that you know that you are enough to be deserving of what you really want. You are moving the locus of control of your life inward and taking your power back. It is a rite of passage that comes with celebration and more than a little bit of trepidation. You are claiming your spiritual adulthood, bidding good-bye to the adolescent culture's patterns of fear, victimhood, and blame. You are claiming your readiness to co-create the future you want, a future in alignment with the greater good. So while you may be making strong statements such as, "Enough GMOs! Enough tar sands! Enough clear-cutting!" what you are really doing is announcing that you are claiming for yourself and others a world in which these things no longer exist. You are holding a vision of what you do want rather than being mired in battles against what you do not. It is easy to miss this important distinction because it is a subtle energetic one. It is why a war on drugs never seems to work. If you want to determine if you are claiming or battling, check in with your emotions. If you feel empowered, optimistic, and grounded, this is claiming. If you are angry or feel indignation, this is battling. Claiming is a very positive feeling because you are also taking back control of your own energy and investing it in co-creating what you *do* want—a world with natural food, clean and renewable energy, and pristine ecosystems.

Claiming the future you want is not about willpower or sacrifice. It is not about becoming your vision right away. It is about choosing a general path or direction. You can eat at a restaurant even while you choose not to buy GMO produce for your household. You can drive a vehicle that uses fossil fuels while you save money to purchase a solar panel for your home. The fulcrum for change is at the level of belief. What are your beliefs about what *should* and *could* be? We get bogged down when we overly focus on what we or others are doing or not doing *right now*. Change is a process. We must be patient and trust our beliefs to guide the pieces in place in right timing for us. What is most important is that we are aware that it is in our power to make a conscious choice. Once our thinking is freed from the Never Enough Story, we've activated the Enough Story. We simply move forward in various areas of our lives as the way clears. There is no need to force or control how or where the Enough future unfolds. It will happen. What is significant is that we have consciously, deliberately chosen. We are on a new trajectory, one we can trust to bring us forward toward the world we want.

Peaceful Activism

It is helpful to keep reminding ourselves that the harmful practices we witness in the world today are a product of the more narrow consciousness of the past, and that narrow consciousness is losing potency on the planet today. It is also losing potency in us. It is inevitable that humanity will eventually see and understand our world from a larger, more systemic and whole perspective than could be accessed from the old Never Enough mindset. Therefore, it will eventually be obvious to almost everyone that the Never Enough practices and systems do not make sense and do not serve the greater good.

Peaceful activists are most needed at this time. This is a very different role than the old model of activism that battled against the status quo. We are learning that confronting someone whose consciousness is stuck in the Never Enough paradigm is a fruitless exercise, because the problem is not one of intelligence (who has the more convincing argument or set of data) but one of worldview.

We know that if you are an environmentalist coming from Transform consciousness of what is best for the planet and are framing your arguments from this viewpoint, you will not reach the person who is perceiving through Gather consciousness (What about my job?), Repeat consciousness (What about my political party?) or Share consciousness (What about my country's sovereignty?) You could try to tailor your argument toward the sphere of interest of each group, but this is still trying to change someone else. So how do you make a difference? How do you catalyze a shift for the better? You would be better off to create from your T level of consciousness, a new, higher trajectory in which you gather (G) with others with a similar consciousness to demonstrate (R) what is possible from your shared level of consciousness so it can be repeated by others and share (S) your models and your successes as broadly as possible, combining resources and people for further progress. You are always acting wisely to spend your energy affiliating with others of like consciousness to create pockets of wholeness where you are, because this way, you are embodying the New Story rather than engaging with or comparing and contrasting the old. As long as a significant part of you is engaged with the old, especially in anger, battle, or blame, you cannot be in full coherence with the new Enough Story. Absolutely leave the door open for others to join you when they are ready, but do not allow yourself to let old consciousness mire or hold back what you are creating.

Enough Is a Field

What I have come to understand is that Enough is much more than an idea or a concept. It is a field of awareness that exists and can be tapped into by any of us. It is a field that has a precise energy, feel, and vibration. Just as you can feel "tension so thick it could be cut with a knife" or a prickling at the back of your neck that alerts you to danger, Enough has a feel of its own that is energetic, optimistic, joyful, empowering, freeing, and abundant. It is loving, nourishing, and peaceful energy that invites connection and co-creativity. To me, Enough is nothing less than my home signal. I know this field is real because I have experienced it, worked with it, transmitted it, and I have seen others embody it as a group with minimal words or explanations. Enough is something we first and foremost feel in our bodies. And it differs from most other vibrational fields we experience because it is not a product of the mind, but emanates directly from our hearts.

Most people today are largely living in their heads, giving their attention to the Never Enough story, which is a collection of thoughts and beliefs such as worrying about not having enough time or money, not feeling secure or loved enough. These thoughts become our personal story line, and when we tell our story over and over again, we take it for truth. It sets into place patterns, ruts, and perceived limitations that do not actually exist outside our own heads. Thoughts based in Never Enough come with a low vibration that is felt as stress, anxiety, fatigue, depression, insecurity, worry, powerlessness, and being in a rut. Most people are so used to the vibration of Never Enough that they unconsciously identify with it as their "normal." The danger comes when we identify so completely with the Never Enough vibration that we can no longer feel our home signal of Enough. As a home signal, Enough is always available to us and always has been. It is a gift on our doorstep, a gift we can give simply by connecting this energy to whatever we do. The more of us who consciously attune to the Enough field even for brief intervals, the more potent it becomes and the easier it becomes to embrace it as our new (and most ancient) normal.

How do we tend the Enough field and share it with others? We do it by "securing our own oxygen mask before assisting others with theirs." We open the door, pick up the gift on our doorstep, and open it up. And then we find ways to keep the Enough Message present in our daily lives. I always recommend starting or joining a circle of people who agree to tend the Enough field of awareness for and with one another. We are building a new culture, a new normal, and this is made exponentially easier with companions who are on the same wavelength, sharing their Enough stories. But even if you are doing this alone, you can keep an Enough journal, tell yourself Enough stories, consider how the most painful experiences in your life would have been experienced differently if you had embraced the awareness that you are enough and the universe is supporting you in every minute to have enough.

When we come together in groups, we tend the Enough field by attuning to our felt sense of group coherence. Whenever we are out of resonance with a group, either because we are not ready or they are not ready, dramas and conflicts arise that seriously slow down the progress of everyone involved. We start to feel pulled from our calm Enough center and back into the Never Enough storm. The dramas and codependent patterns of caretaking and second-guessing distract us from doing the important work that needs to be done for the world. For this reason, it is more important than ever to exercise discernment when forming or stewarding a group.

Having the right skillset or job experience is no longer the primary factor for group success. Group resonance is. When any group member notices a rise in drama, conflict, or a lack of resonance in the group, it is imperative that he or she alerts the group. More than protecting fragile egos or avoiding conflict, we must make it a priority to protect and improve group coherence. Never Enough vibrations feel like someone sucked all the air out of the room, the floor dropped out from under an uplifting, inspiring conversation, or there is a fog, confusion, or turbulence rumbling just under the surface. When we feel this in a group or in ourselves, it is our responsibility to pause, to go into silence, and to tap into the Enough field, asking, What does Enough look like in this situation? Is Never Enough thinking impinging on coherence? How can we help others in our group to tap into their home Enough signal instead of responding through habits of fear and lack?

We are creating a new kind of activism with our choices. Because Never Enough has been the human operating system for so long, Enough is a vibration we have to actually choose.

For a time, we must remember to claim our enoughness over and over again. The good news is that it will not be long before it becomes our new normal with no effort at all. I noticed the start of the transition from effort to effortlessness while listening to the television coverage of the Pope and President Barack Obama addressing the United Nations. I could not only hear but deeply feel in my heart the Enough vibration as they implored people to care for Earth and to embrace others as ourselves. I was near tears almost the whole time. But in contrast, the news anchors and pundits brought the conversation energetically much lower both leading up to and after the speeches, feeling the need to inject drama and suspense. Everything they were saying was rooted in Never Enough scarcity, fear, blame, and separation.

I could feel my heart close and my anger, disappointment, and frustration rise. It would be tempting to dwell in those lower emotions, but I caught myself, asking how I'd rather feel and what I'd rather project into the world. As a result, I carried with me throughout my day the feeling of hope and unity. In the past, I would have felt compelled to share the lower vibration story of my disappointment in the journalists. I realize they are just complying with a pattern that many journalists share the world over. They are not inherently evil or primitive. As the audience evolves, the media's approach will shift in kind.

I am also noticing the shift toward effortlessness through my closest relationships. It appears as a new intolerance for emotional gamesmanship, including passive aggressiveness, martyrdom, and assumptions of entitlement. As a classic people pleaser, I used to fall for all of these, but now I seem to possess a new immunity and resilience that allows me to avoid them. I simply choose not to play.

The greatest service we can give to the planet right now is to keep our energy and consciousness clean and clear. When we refuse to play Never Enough games and take claim to our enoughness, it should be fun and rewarding because we are liv-ing purposefully and serving the greater good with our inner gifts. We are co-creating new Enough ground for others to stand on. This is quite different from either falling for or fighting against the old Never Enough structures. It is not productive to shame or blame the people who still want to play the old game. We must honor the free will, choice, and sovereignty of every human being. But we certainly can change the world by focusing our attention where it builds the Enough future we do want.

I want to be clear. There is absolutely a place for standing up to say no to something that is harmful or unjust. But can you imagine how much more empowering our participation in a protest or rally would be if you knew you were already creating and claiming what you *do* want? Can you see how you come to the rally as an empowered being, not as a victim pleading for change? You *are* the change already. You have exited the perpetrator-hero-victim story. You bring the pioneering energy of clarity, faith, vision, and solidarity with you, and those energies are powerful and magnetic. It is with this power of knowing who you are that you can truly, commandingly say, "Enough!" and be heard.

Not a Handout or a Hand Up but Hand in Hand

In her book *Urgent Message from Mother*, Jean Shinoda Bolen shares a story that demonstrates the powerful shift from victim to empowered change agent. A woman in a village in Uganda was married to a physically abusive husband. The other women in the village became very concerned, so they went to her to ask how they could help. She eventually agreed to accept help and the women came up with a plan. They gave her a plastic pennywhistle to put around her neck and asked her to blow the whistle whenever her husband started to beat her. When they heard the whistle, the women ran into her house and each stood before the husband and said, "Beat *me*. Beat *me*." He was so mortified that he stopped. Eventually, all the women in the village wore whistles. They took the whistles to other villages, and then other villages, with the same results. Eventually, Uganda passed a bill to make spousal abuse illegal.

The story of the whistleblowers from Uganda demonstrates what activism looks like in an emerging Enough world. The women could have remained in the perpetrator-hero-victim story as victims, feeling powerless and doing nothing ("we are not enough to affect change"). They could have risen as heroes to try to turn the man (the perpetrator) into the authorities. They could have pooled their money to help the woman and her children to escape to a new life, which may solve this one woman's problem but would do nothing to alter the conditions by which abuse is accepted as "just the way things are." They could have done any number of things to offer a *hand out* or a *hand up* to their friend in distress. What they did instead was to stand with her *hand in hand*. By choosing to stand together in a public way, they were shifting the culture and proclaiming not that "this man is bad" but that "we stand for a culture in which spousal abuse is not acceptable." Their action did not reinforce patterns of separation or shame by stepping in as heroes or accusers. Instead they all chose to stand as one to claim the Enough future they all wanted. As a result, they advanced their vision for how the world could and should be, not only for their friend and their village, but for their entire country.

Solutionaries

When we engage those we'd formerly only consider "victims" as part of the solution—as primary program designers, change agents, and activists—and we welcome their wisdom, skills, sovereignty, and creativity, we can expect much better outcomes to arise from that synergy. The Institute for Humane Education (IHE) uses the term "solutionary," which I love because it elegantly combines the attributes of solutions, visionary, and evolutionary. IHE is partnering with educators to shift the paradigm in education, helping children to see themselves as the empowered solutionaries the world needs. They operate a school for educators that shares lesson plans developed by their graduates.

Their plans include solutionary congresses to bring this new paradigm directly to school-age children.

Girl Effect, an organization that empowers girls in poverty, is another example of this. Embedded in all their materials is a commitment to involve girls in the planning, to ask what they need, and to not make assumptions or charge in with preconceived solutions. Combining activism with participative leadership ensures we are truly listening to what is being asked for and what is not. It ensures that givers and receivers are seen as partners who are simply bringing different sets of resources and knowledge to the task of creating a mutually desired outcome. *Hand in hand* is empowering and enlivening for everyone.

Group Synergy Gives Us Access to the Whole

We know our genius goes much deeper than our IQs. We know that when we come together essence to essence, we generate a shared field of synergistic intelligence, a new kind of multisensory genius that includes what we access through the seeing of the heart and our connection to the Zero Point Field. From this place of greater awareness and connection, our insights and our decisions are naturally harmonious, peaceful, and more whole. The ego takes its proper place, serving the greater good and not running the show. Individuals are seen as precious and unique, but, at the same time, narcissism and competition are not fed nor is selfishness or hero worship. As we enter the adulthood of the human species, we think systemically, seeing our processes always as being connected to everything else, imbued with mature responses of reciprocity and doing least harm. We understand that one of the gifts of community is that it gives each individual greater access to the whole picture.

At the 2013 United Nations Commission on the Status of Women, Ambassador Anwarul K. Chowdhury, who is arguably one of the most effective advocates for women's rights the United Nations has ever seen, gave a truly inspiring speech to a small group of us who were gathered together by Jean Shinoda

Bolen. He stated that the biggest problem in changing the United Nations in terms of women's rights is the UN culture itself that tends to only see women as victims. He believed that so much more could be accomplished if instead those at the UN perceived women as people with valuable information, resources, and solutions.

In many cultures, women are the primary weavers of village life. They know their communities inside and out and have formed resilient networks of mutual aid and communion. So often, a group of foreign experts comes in from outside, not understanding the culture and having no established trust or relationships in the communities they are seeking to serve. Instead of asking what is most needed or how they could partner with existing efforts, they bypass the existing community networks, impose a solution, and then are surprised that when they leave their efforts are not carried on.

I heard many stories like this while at the UN conference. Women were pleading with the representatives to consult with them about how best to solve the problems in their communities. "We know how to solve our problems," the women would say in various accents or through translators. "We lack the critical resources you could provide, but we know what needs to be done already. We can mobilize the community. Why aren't you involving us?" I saw this same frustration echoed by the various grassroots groups in attendance. These groups would present data that proved great successes achieved on shoestring budgets. Bureaucrats were in their own meetings literally across the hall or across the street. The grassroots groups would ask, "Why aren't you sending anyone over to learn from us? We're right here. We know how to solve the problems efficiently and cheaply. Come learn from us. Let's work together."

Many grassroots groups model hand in hand. But our political structures are products of the Never Enough paradigm, tending to repeat perpetrator-victim-hero patterns and prejudices. Through the eyes of the old patriarchy, outstretched hands of ordinary caring citizens are not perceived as partnership or opportunity but as a challenge to the established order.

My point in bringing up the divide between the hero story and the grassroots operating system is not to add to the anger and frustration I have witnessed, but to provide encouragement to the grassroots to just keep moving forward. It is not necessary to involve those with deep pockets or sanctioned power. Your achievements for now may be constrained by shoestring budgets, but what you are building together by staying unfettered by the bureaucracy and red tape is so much more. It is easy to believe we don't have enough and aren't doing enough. But maybe we actually do and are. We are contending with the inertia of overlapping paradigms, and that often feels like wading through molasses. But we deny our own power when we believe we aren't enough to move forward on our own, that we need the money, permission, or stamp of approval of the old paradigm in order to move forward. We may believe the support of the old bureaucracy could speed things up for us, but the reality could just as likely be that it could slow us down. So often, these kinds of opportunities come with undesirable parameters and strings. Being light and lean is a big asset in times of rapid change like this.

We aren't victims. We aren't powerless. We are solutionaries engaged in changing the world. We should be loud and proud about what we've accomplished. We should share our stories far and wide. This is how we will attract the attention of the people who have ears to hear us, people whose hearts sing the same song, people who gladly support us without needing to control or take credit for what we are doing.

Telling Our Enough Stories

There is an old Never Enough imbalance that we tend to bring with us into the new: the imbalance between doing and reflecting. The core assumption is that there isn't enough time for reflection. This imbalance manifests in grassroots groups that are so busy trying to change the world they forget to take the time to share their stories. As we move from one paradigm to the next, the importance of storytelling becomes an absolutely critical piece. The world is starving for stories of hope and possibility from the newly forming paradigm. Our hearts are so parched for meaning and connection. A good story can awaken our hearts and leave us looking for more that feeds this part of us. We become magnetically drawn to efforts that align with our vision for a better world.

Who will provide this nourishment? We all could. We could commit to spending more of our time sharing the good news, the success stories, the heart-opening stories and showing people what is possible from an Enough mindset. Some ways to do this are to work in short sabbaticals to our schedules or to designate someone as the group's storyteller, blogger, videographer, or journalist. In the age of social media, our stories, whether as videos, blogs, memes, or tweets, have never had a larger impact and reach. I would suggest that the time we used to spend trying to enlist the support of the old system could be better invested in storytelling, with much greater results. We are in the business of awakening hearts. It is the heart that feels the call of our stories of community, compassion, and empowerment most strongly right now. It is the heart that will resonate with good news and become activated to take action. Our siren call, then, is not directed at the old power structures built by heads without hearts, but at those who have already begun awakening. Open hearts can receive what we are offering, precious nourishment in the form of authenticity, truth, caring, and deep meaningfulness.

The power of social media also means that participation in hand in hand action can be as swift as the click of a button. Organizations like *www.Change.org*, and Care2 offer do-it-yourself petition-making tools. A signed petition is something any activist can use to say, "I don't stand alone. See?" Crowdfunding platforms provide direct donor-to-receiver funding, a way to pool resources, and proof that even a very little bit from each person can add up to more than enough. For example, HopeMob, a crowdfunding platform, attracted a half million donors in its first six months, donating 100 percent of what they received directly to the causes they support. What organizers are finding is that when they create a way for people to join together around a dream for the future, people are eager to participate.

Love Moves Us Forward in the Direction of Our Dream

As the many new online charitable platforms reveal, it is not necessary to use blame, shame, or fear to motivate people to take action that contributes to the greater good. That was the old Never Enough way, and it rarely worked as a sustainable strategy because people are wired to avoid facing the pain and fear inherent in these stories. When the attractor is instead a dream for a better world, people show up and give because they want to experience a sense of hope, meaning, connection, and purpose. This inner motivation is inherent and can be trusted. It doesn't need to be coerced, shamed, or shocked into being. People give because it opens their hearts and makes them feel *good*. Civic engagement and philanthropy don't need to mean angry, sad, or loud. We can stand together, hand in hand, creating a space for something to emerge that we can love into being together.

Peace and well-being come from forgiveness, from abandoning the illusion that we can hate and not suffer from carrying the emotion of hate within ourselves. Peace and well-being come from aligning with love. Self-love asks for this. When we know we are enough, when we cultivate that self-love, we know we are worthy of such a world. Martin Luther King, Jr. and Mahatma Gandhi modeled for us the way of the peaceful warrior by not returning hate with hate, but by turning instead to the power and beauty of our dreams. They invited us to turn fists into outreached hands and screams of outrage into prayers of hope and songs of connection. King put it this way:

When I speak of love I am not speaking of some sentimental and weak response which is little more than emotional bosh. I am speaking of that force which all of the great religions have seen as the supreme unifying principle of life. Love is somehow the key that unlocks the door which leads to ultimate reality.

Loving our dreams transforms us, especially the kind of love that comes from within when we believe we are enough to make our dreams come true.

Part Three

Invocation of the New Story

❧ 10 ❧

The Enough Story Has Begun!

It is never too late to embrace the kind of world you want to live in.
Any time you are ready is the right time.

When my son was taking piano lessons as a small boy, I learned that when you press one key on a piano, all the keys on the piano of the same letter (such as a C) slightly vibrate with it, as if being awakened by some invisible connection between them. This phenomenon is known as resonance. I believe resonance is in operation all over the universe as the siren call to humanity. Enough is hitting a certain key, and those who vibrate with it are simultaneously awakening and finding one another through some kind of mutual felt resonance. This is a new note arising in us, a breakthrough vibration.

In his groundbreaking work on the vibrational frequency of emotions, David R. Hawkins, MD, PhD, quantified the vibrational frequency of various human emotions, placing them on a scale very much like the keys of a piano. Joy, for example, is one of the highest frequency emotions, with guilt and shame at the very bottom of the scale (yes, well below anger and fear). Observing how our bodies feel and what we attract when feeling various emotions can be quite instructive and empowering when we realize our role as co-creators. If we spend a great deal of time feeling low-vibration emotions such as guilt, shame, anger, or fear, we know we are orienting primarily toward the old Never Enough Story. As we experience increasing joy, love, peace, and acceptance, we move into Enough territory. The emotional hooks and dramas that used to dominate our lives fail to draw us in as we commit to fostering a higher, cleaner frequency.

As a result of altering our frequencies, we may start to feel like outsiders to our old identities, roles, stories, dramas, and patterns, too light somehow to be caught up in their familiar but heavy web of complication and repetition. Our tastes may suddenly change. Relationships may end or transform. Activities that used to bring us pleasure no longer do. We may find ourselves shifting from introvert to extrovert, or perhaps the opposite, shifting from extrovert to introvert. Many women who have been mostly complacent about how the world has operated for decades in the hands of men may find they feel compelled to speak out powerfully and with authority at this time.

Let it flow. All this is normal in the shift. It means we are truly unplugging from the Old Story and finding the real escape route rather than getting stuck in old ruts of pain, suffering, and fear. We are becoming more whole, and whole means being drawn to the parts of ourselves that have been kept in a relatively unexpressed state for a long time.

When we feel this disorientation, we don't need to worry that we are somehow losing our identity. The old, familiar parts of ourselves that we want to keep cannot be lost. The parts of us that were suppressed by the Never Enough paradigm are coming forward to have their turn to be expressed now. We are not losing our minds or having a midlife crisis. We are shedding denser beliefs and regaining our freedom to step into more wholeness.

Integration—Becoming the Change

On the day I received the Enough Message, I experienced a benevolent, loving, and incredibly sparkling energy coming from a source I perceived at the time to be outside of myself. What has happened over the course of three years is that this energy has gently and gradually penetrated my cells and dissolved into my essence, becoming part of me. Integration of new ideas and beliefs takes time. For me, integration has taken place through several well-paced Enough initiations, situations in which I was presented with a difficult choice to either align with Enough or Never Enough beliefs about myself and the world. When I chose Not Enough, I found that I would receive feedback from my body almost instantly. I would develop a migraine or stomachache. I would feel my body's aches and pains more intensely.

Each time I chose Enough, my life got lighter and better. I felt more energy surging through me and received more inspiration. Synchronicities would increase. Each time I recommitted to living my Enough life, it accelerated the delivery of what I wanted.

My friend Gus used to say that the universe "ups the ante" each time we revisit a pattern and choose the path that does not honor our truths. By this, he means that it is more painful each time we willingly remain entrenched in our old ways. Perhaps at first we were unclear about the choice at hand, but by repeating a pattern, more light is shed on our decision. Enough always represents the natural universal flow, the world without the stories that make us act in ways that are out of alignment with our true wants and needs. We can simply ask, "If I knew for sure that I am precious and enough as I am, what choice would I make?" Or we could simply feel our way: "Which choice in this situation makes me feel more peaceful and calm? Which makes me nervous or uneasy?" I call this the soft belly test, because we can observe this difference directly in our bellies. Using muscle testing is another way to access the body's reliable wisdom and to align with our Enough Story.

I am understanding the phrase "be the change" at a more profound level than ever before. It means standing up boldly for our inner truth—especially when it contradicts old established patterns. It means trusting our growing edge. It means welcoming Enough initiations and observing the expansion of enoughness within us that happens after. I am living increasingly in an Enough Story now, understanding that an Enough world is not separate from who we are, but is a field that permeates everything, including ourselves. As students of a Newtonian materialism, we have mistakenly perceived ourselves as solid, separate, and rather unchangeable beings of limited potential. But we know now this is not nearly the whole story of who we are or could be. The Newtonian view concentrated only on an infinitesimal part of who we are, the .0001 percent represented by solid matter. There is much more room to expand into. 99.999

percent more room. This is the territory where we can expect leaps of understanding, genius, communion, magic, and miracles. This much energy and possibility is certainly hard to grasp. It can certainly take some getting used to.

From an Enough perspective, I see that the old me was a much more constricted person—constricted by self-selected fears, self-doubt, excuses, habits, can't and don't, what I perceived I should be, and the belief that the future cannot possibly be that much different from the past. When that person shows up (and she does still show up, but thankfully less often), I greet her with compassion, reminding her that although she may have thought those old choices made her safe, they actually disempowered her and perpetuated the kind of world she did not want to live in. I remind her that the world we want doesn't just happen to us. We must claim it through our choices, one by one.

It is important to note that we did not always have the freedom to select the kind of planetary future we can today. This window of opportunity is new. The Never Enough illusion was for a very long time too convincing, the walls of distortion too thick. But the walls have been crumbling. Much more light is shining through the cracks. Some people have broken through to the other side and are bringing back vivid tales from the new territory. We no longer can use the excuse that the signposts and visions are not there. We can look to pioneers such as Margaret Wheatley and Lynne McTaggart for the intersection of quantum science, consciousness, and leadership; Rachel Carson, Frances Moore Lappé, Joanna Macy, and Bill McKibben for the conscious breakthrough of ecospirituality; Bruce Lipton and Jill Bolte Taylor for new understandings about consciousness and brain science; Elisabet Sahtouris for the New Story implications of evolutionary biology; Jean Shinoda Bolen, Llewellyn Vaughan-Lee, Andrew Harvey, and Riane Eisler for feminine forms of leadership; Charles Eisenstein and James O'Dea for sacred economics and sacred activism; and Buckminster

Fuller, Jean Houston, Barbara Marx Hubbard, and Marianne Williamson as mentors for conscious evolution and revolution.

Key insights have been offered by poets and artists such as Rumi, John Lennon, and Drew Dellinger, by the indigenous wisdom keepers and by spiritual leaders such as the Dalai Lama, Pope Francis, Pema Chödrön, Matthew Fox, and Thich Nhat Hanh. Humanity is hungry for a unified cosmology, a mission stewarded brilliantly by expansive thinkers such as Albert Einstein, Brian Swimme, Thomas Berry, David Korten, Rupert Sheldrake, Ken Wilbur, Gregory Bateson, and Ervin László. Each of these human beings and so many more eloquently express the story of wholeness, of integrating many disciplines into a totally new understanding of the world.

Our present-day opportunity to invent the world anew has been built on millennia of painstaking learning, doing, reflecting, and clearing. We need to appreciate the tremendous amount of work that has gone into making this moment of transition possible for us, honoring the dedication of the billions of people who have come before us and the billions of people who join us now at this very special time in planetary, galactic, and cosmic history.

We Are the Choice Makers

The question for us is not if but *when* this shift will take hold of planetary human culture. We can have it in our lifetime. We can ride the wave of change in any way we like. We can cling to the old shore and experience the pain of the breakdown a while longer. Or we can perch ourselves boldly on the leading edge and be one of the first to wash up on the Enough shore. The point is, we who are present on the planet today get to choose. This has not been the case for over five thousand years.

If I have done my duty to the Enough Message, I will have provided adequate information to encourage you to jump into the mystery a little earlier than you otherwise would have. If I have been a clear translator, I will have helped you to see that your impulses are guided and supported by a meta-story of truly cosmic proportions and that this story is already spreading like wildflowers globally in the form of all the social movements and innovations that are arising from this shared impulse.

It is impossible for me to put into words the preciousness of what is opening to us now, but the Enough Message provided what I believe is a decent hint: *Together we rise!* I wouldn't want anyone to deny him- or herself a single moment of the enjoyment that awaits in the New Story. I am not an expert, nor do I aspire to be one. I cannot advise you on what to do or when. I cannot predict your future. Only you know what feels right for you. What I do know is that we will determine the future together through our individual heart-guided choices and efforts. I can tell you that what you choose matters much more than you could imagine, not only to you but to future generations and to the planet. It is our time to be bold, to trust our hearts, and to let go of the shore.

I can tell you that I have made my choice. Writing this book is the tangible evidence of having chosen a very different path than I've been used to. At fifty-one, an age I have been told should be about settling into my ways and sitting back, I am taking bigger risks and speaking up in bolder ways. This choice to be different and to act more boldly has meant feeling significantly vulnerable and uncomfortable at times. Most often what was making me uncomfortable was to venture beyond the places where I used to always stop myself. I simply didn't know what would happen if I ignored the authoritative voice inside that said I was not enough to make a difference or that there was danger in being my big self. But the strength to step forward this time doesn't come from "mustering courage" but from sensing that I am on a very big team that as a whole cannot fail. The universal Enough Story gives me strength and resolve I could never have imagined. Even if I were to fail, I know the larger Enough impetus that is here now on our planet will not fail. Our story is already written.

Nothing from within the Old Story can predict our personal calling in the New Story. The transformation from caterpillar to butterfly teaches that there is no straight line from one story to the next. We must expect surprises and the seemingly miraculous as we transition from Share to Transform and from Never Enough to Enough. We can no longer hold back with excuses that we are not qualified to do the work of a planetary change agent. The Enough paradigm is truly a different territory and doesn't operate by linear rules. It honors and respects spontaneous arisings and does not require credentials, personal recommendations, or résumés. All of this is to say that you can do whatever calls to you and it will be beautifully, perfectly enough.

It is never too late to embrace the Enough world you want to live in. Anytime you are ready is the right time.

Invocation

My choice is to belong to an Enough world.
I can be content with no other.
It is that simple.
And it is simple to know what to do now.
I will share Enough stories.
I will spread love notes.
And I promise to listen intently for yours.
In the end,
I feel certain that for each of us,
And for the world,
That will surely be enough.

Acknowledgments

Years ago, I learned about the South African philosophy of *ubuntu*, which translates roughly to "I am because you are." Anything that we do is possible only because we are embedded in a web of interconnection. When we know this web is the truth of the universe, the truth of who *we* are, we realize that we are not and never have been separate individuals. When our name is spoken, it does not refer only to us as a separate personality. It includes the sum total of all the love, wisdom, and support we have received; the sum total of all the challenges, conflicts, and trials that have honed us through the years. We are a ripple in a pond as well as the interactions of all the ripples in the pond. We are never alone—not even when we act individually, such as putting pen to paper with the intention of writing a book. It is with this understanding of ubuntu that I share my gratitude with the following people:

My tireless champion, Caroline Pincus at Conari, where I have been the beneficiary of the supreme talent and dedication of the entire Conari team: Caroline Pincus, Jan Johnson, Bonni Hamilton, Eryn Carter, Jim Warner, Jane Hagaman, and Susie Pitzen.

I am forever awed and humbled by the gifts of circle and the importance of women as soul evolvers at this important time in planetary history. I wish to thank my first writer's circle: my mother and Linda Hogan for nurturing every stage of the writing process; and my women's circle: Deborah Tallarico, Cara Forte, Jen Fox, Annie Finch, Cindy Heelan, Judy Violette, and Pam Florea for holding a powerful field of unconditional love and trustworthiness for both me and the world. I am forever indebted to Cheryl Gould and Ann Landaas Smith for showing up as midwives at the birth of the Enough Message, to Ann Landaas Smith (again) and Jean Shinoda Bolen for partnering with me at the fledgling stages of the Enough work, and to the Conveners' Circle of Gather the Women for saying yes to my first Enough teleseries. To my dear and precious close friends, various angels and guides, both seen and unseen, for your love and support and for showing up at key points along my Enough journey to remind me to stay faithful to my assignment. (You know who you are!)

I wish to express my deepest gratitude to my beautiful family: to my mother Joan Candelmo, a teacher, children's book writer, and illustrator, for loving me so purely and completely all the days of my life and for being the very model of the Sovereign I describe; to my sister Terri Eddy, an environmental advocate, for her precious friendship and lifelong example of making the world a better place through service and education; to my father Phil Candelmo, a writer and entrepreneur, for teaching me it is worth it to take risks and for never hesitating to show up with unconditional love when I've needed him; to my soul sister Linda Hogan, a social architect and courageous visionary, who more times than I could ever count has held me steady as I straddled the old and new worlds, and whose wisdom, in the form of thousands of sacred conversations, reverberates throughout this entire book; to my thoughtful and gifted son Chris McCammon, who has fulfilled and surpassed countless wishes and who shows me every day that the future is in supremely capable hands. I especially wish to acknowledge my beloved husband Joe McCammon, whose grounding love and care have made possible a steady foundation of Enough in every aspect for me and our family for twenty-five beautiful years.

May my embrace be large enough to be felt by all of you.

I am because you are.

Bibliography

Baldwin, Christina. *Calling the Circle: The First and Future Culture*. New York: Bantam, 1998.

Baldwin, Christina, and Ann Linnea. *The Circle Way: A Leader in Every Chair*. San Francisco: Berrett-Koehler, 2010.

Bolen, Jean Shinoda. *Urgent Message from Mother: Gather the Women, Save the World*. San Francisco: Conari Press, 2008.

Bolte Taylor, Jill. *My Stroke of Insight: A Brain Scientist's Personal Journey*. New York: Penguin, 2006.

Estés, Clarissa Pinkola. *Women Who Run With the Wolves: Myths and Stories of the Wild Woman Archetype*. New York: Ballantine, 1996.

Hawken, Paul. *Blessed Unrest: How the Largest Social Movement in History Is Restoring Grace, Justice, and Beauty to the World*. New York: Penguin, 2008.

Hawkins, David R. *Power Versus Force: An Anatomy of Consciousness, the Hidden Determinants of Human Behavior*. Carlsbad, CA: Hay House, 2013.

Helman, Christopher. "The World's Happiest (And Saddest) Countries, 2013," Forbes, October 29, 2013, http://www.forbes.com/sites/christopherhelman/2013/10/29/the-worlds-happiest-and-saddest-countries-2013/.

Hemenway, Toby. "The History & Legacy of Agriculture," August 26, 2012, https://www.youtube.com/watch?v=UFWdbfo_m0s.

Jaccaci, August T. *General Periodicity: Nature's Creative Dynamics*. Scarborough, ME: Fiddlehead, 2000.

Jaccaci, August T., and Susan B. Gault. *CEO: Chief Evolutionary Officer—Leaders Mapping the Future*. Woburn, MA: Butterworth-Heinemann, 1999.

Koestler, Arthur. *The Ghost in the Machine*. New York: Penguin, 1990.

Land, George. *Grow or Die: The Unifying Principle of Transformation*. Carlsbad, CA: Leadership 2000, 1997.

Lappé, Frances Moore. *EcoMind: Changing the Way We Think, to Create the World We Want*. New York: Nation Books, 2011.

Liedloff, Jean. *The Continuum Concept: In Search of Happiness Lost*. New York: Perseus Books, 1986.

McTaggart, Lynne. *The Field: The Quest for the Secret Force of the Universe*. New York: Harper Perennial, 2008.

"Murmuration." YouTube via Islands & Rivers, October 26, 2011, https://vimeo.com/31158841.

Sahtouris, Elisabet. "Towards a Future Global Science: Axioms for Modeling a Living Universe," December 2008, http://www.sahtouris.com/pdfs/WFRArticle2008.pdf.

Senge, Peter. *The Fifth Discipline: The Art & Practice of the Learning Organization*. New York: Doubleday, 2006.

Straub, Gail. *Returning to My Mother's House: Taking Back the Wisdom of the Feminine*. West Hurley, NY: High Point, 2008.

Tolle, Eckhart. *A New Earth: Awakening to Your Life's Purpose*. New York: Penguin, 2008.

Weil, Zoe. "The World Becomes What You Teach" TEDxDirigo, January 14, 2011, https://www.youtube.com/watch?v=t5HEV96dIuY.

Williamson, Marianne. *A Return to Love: Reflections on the Principles of A Course in Miracles*. San Francisco: HarperOne, 1996.

About the Author

 Laurie McCammon, founder of the Women's Institute of Maine, holds an MS in Adult Education, with a thesis on transformational learning. She has served as an NGO delegate at the UN International Commission on the Status of Women where she presented *Enough!* in 2013 and 2014. She has been published in numerous magazines including *Soulful Living, Inner Awakenings, Spiritual Renaissance*, and *Allies for the Greater Good*. Visit her at *www.weareenough.com*.

To Our Readers

Conari Press, an imprint of Red Wheel/Weiser, publishes books on topics ranging from spirituality, personal growth, and relationships to women's issues, parenting, and social issues. Our mission is to publish quality books that will make a difference in people's lives—how we feel about ourselves and how we relate to one another. We value integrity, compassion, and receptivity, both in the books we publish and in the way we do business.

Our readers are our most important resource, and we appreciate your input, suggestions, and ideas about what you would like to see published.

Visit our website at *www.redwheelweiser.com* to learn about our upcoming books and free downloads, and be sure to go to *www.redwheelweiser.com/newsletter* to sign up for newsletters and exclusive offers.

You can also contact us at *info@rwwbooks.com*.
Conari Press
an imprint of Red Wheel/Weiser, llc
65 Parker Street, Suite 7
Newburyport, MA 01950